Trish Deseine

Photography by Marie-Pierre Morel

nobody does it better...

Why French home cooking is still the best in the world

Kyle Cathie Limited

Pour Louisette, Dona, Marie-Laure, Anne-Marie, Noël et Odile, the Frenchwomen who taught me to cook. Personne ne fait mieux.

First published in Great Britain in 2007 by
Kyle Cathie Limited
122 Arlington Road
London NW1 7HP
www.kylecathie.com

ISBN 978 1 85626 616 1

Editorial director **Muna Reyal**
Designed by **Mary Evans**
Photography by **Marie-Pierre Morel** except for pages 12, 23, 39, 52 right, 65, 70 top left and right, 83, 84 bottom left, 118, 119 by **Sylvain Thomas** and page 6 by **Deirdre Rooney**
Food styling by **Trish Deseine**
Styling by **Pauline Ricard-Andre**
Copyediting by **Marion Moisy**
Junior Editor **Danielle Di Michiel**
Production by **Sha Huxtable** and **Alice Holloway**

Colour reproduction by Sang Choy
Printed by TWP in Singapore

Introduction **6**

Shops wisely **15**

Knows her classics **107**

Steals from chefs **171**

Rises to the occasion **195**

Until a few years ago, most French cookery books were all about HOW TO COOK PROPERLY and were produced by chefs with two to three Michelin stars, more committed to sharing their great knowledge gathered through years of hard toil than prefacing their books with childhood memories.

introduction

Being France, of course, cooking was explained, not explored. It was intellectualised in books but rarely expressed from a personal, anecdotal, or nostalgic viewpoint. For why state the obvious? Why share 'personal' experiences so widespread as to be practically universal? To your average French chef, uncovering the reasons for their choice of *métier* is as relevant as an Englishman finding childhood inspiration for his love of cricket. An unnecessary dismantling of traditional life.

As an Irish writer of French cookery books, I have recently found myself on something of a mission to reverse this trend. As an untrained home cook and working mother, my books are not intellectual or formal; they try to be pragmatic and personal. My thought was to try to make my readers want to cook rather than telling them how to. There is a saying in French, '*nul n'est prophète dans son propre pays*' – no man is a prophet in his own country. Sometimes we accept advice more easily when it comes from an outsider. The deep affection the French hold for Ireland is a large part of the reason why defensive French cooks will take on board what a non professional has to say, and why they don't feel threatened by stories about themselves.

My conversion to the French culinary religion started on a third-form school trip to Paris. It was a holiday that was memorable for the wrong reasons, ill supervised by three teachers, all just as excited by the prospect of fleeing parents and spouses as tasting the cultural joys of the world's most beautiful city.

The food didn't disappoint: the croissants and *pain au chocolat* which I spread thick with butter (unsalted!) and jam were as rich as in my dreams, the *saucisson* redolent with old garlic I would reel at today and studded with nose-popping pepper, the steak and chips exotically familiar. I had never tasted anything like it.

But my particular life-as-food moment happened unexpectedly in a self-service *cafétéria* on Boulevard St Michel as my first *petit suisse* (small, round cheese) rolled out of its soggy paper into the little heap of sugar awaiting it. Even before trying its salt-sweet-sourness, I was fascinated by how much effort had gone into keeping those two mouthfuls moist and in shape. In the end I can't say I really LIKED the taste or the texture. But I was overcome by the fascination I felt for a people who would go so far for apparently so little.

From then on my palate seemed programmed to embrace everything edible and Gallic. Paris had worked its magic. I was already giddily in schoolgirl love with my bow-tied French teacher, Mr Snowball. It all fell into place. At 13, my future was France and its food.

Further confirmation came at 18, during my first holiday job. Whilst my classmates simply did the Duke of Edinburgh award, I was sent to appreciate how much my parents had done for me by working in the kitchen and laundry of a *hotel de passe* in Vendée. So naïve was I, and so poor was my French, that it took me ten confusing days to work out the link between the *routiers* (lorry drivers) who ate the fantastically fresh and cheap food I helped prepare and the over-made-up women constantly riding the lift of my apartment block across the road.

Work started at 7am. Every day at 11.30 before the customers arrived, I got to eat the melons, tomatoes, cucumbers and salads I had transformed into *entrées du jour*, *tomates farcies*, *concombres à la crème*, *céleri remoulade*, *melon au porto*. This nearly made up for the hellish time I assumed I was jolly well meant to be having. But I finally, tearfully, complained after a Godfather moment when the sadistic chef, knowing how we Irish strangely worship the beasts uncooked, presented me with a horse's head on a tray.

My mortified mother immediately had me whisked away to more genteel surroundings. I was taken in by Madame Adorable Family, whose generous first instinct was to sit me down in front of a huge bowl of barely cooled langoustines. The pleasure I took in their sweetness combined with eggy, mustardy home-made mayonnaise made me feel far more grown up than anything I had learned so far.

She taught me to cook a little, but more importantly, how to entertain *à la française*. A few years later when I moved to Paris with my French *amoureux*, equipped with academic Français and a culinary inferiority complex as solid as my appetite, I at least already had a basic knowledge of how to stage lunch or dinner before a French gathering. Cooking for my French family turned out to be the best way I found to win acceptance by them. The way to his heart turned out to be through his family's stomachs.

French guests always expected the food to be awful. If it was, that was no surprise, and if it wasn't, well, it was a triumph. I put so much emotion, so many dreams and expectations into everything I cooked at first that meals were inevitably transformed into mountains of self-inflicted pressure. I copied my French girlfriends and developed all sorts of stratagems to maintain my cool whilst keeping guests happy. But, unlike them, my all-embracing love of French food meant I would behave like a child in a toy shop every time I bought the groceries. Everything was new, delicious and crying out to be tried. And so I tried and I tried: blueberry pies in Grenoble, foie gras soup in Bordeaux, dry cider in Morlaix, *flameküche* in Strasbourg.

Fast-forwarding through 15 years of culinary discovery, trials, victories and disappointments, one day I was asked by a French publisher to share with French readers my experiences, creations and (what had become) relaxed attitude to cooking in a cookery book and I found myself with a new career.

So why do the French do it better?

The onslaught of other cuisines on the world's tastebuds may have deflated France's national culinary grandeur at restaurant level. But French current-of-life cooking, the stuff you and I do every day, remains supreme. The superlative daily meal is still being set firmly, again and again, on a French table.

Because the French cook enjoys an unparalleled range of sophistication in her cooking, dipping with confidence into all levels of that famously rich pyramid of French cooking. From its solid base of popular dishes, right through the *bistro* and *brasserie* fare, up to starred chefs' airy *haute cuisine*, each level is further enriched with ever-evolving regional variety. Her repertoire is myriad, at once inspired and innate, from artery-blocking fat to fresh-from-the-sea-that-day healthy. Trendily ethnic or traditionally *terroir*. All that and still wonderfully, completely French.

A Frenchwoman knows her classic dishes but does not get stuck in the past, however glorious or regionally appropriate it may be. She will embrace new trends to happily tweak and update old staples. A French cook shops with care and passion in the fabulous variety of specialist shops, markets, delis and supermarkets available.

With a little curiosity and energy we can similiarly connect to traditional cooking in the UK. As standards and demand and enjoyment rise, farmers' markets and specialist shops are springing up, and more and more cookery books are appearing, explaining and revitalising British and Irish cooking. It is now easy to look back proudly to a few generations past when most meals were cooked from scratch with local ingredients and start doing just that again.

The French cook knows how to rise to the occasion when a little extra spending and theatricality are called for. She considers it quite normal to steal and adapt the latest ideas from restaurant chefs, but would never imagine announcing to her guests as she brings a dish to the table, 'this is Raymond's *tourte de blettes*'. These simple principles come naturally to the French, but not to us. I hope that through the stories and recipes of the French cooks who have taught me so much you will absorb some of their know-how, take a more uninhibited attitude to feeding yourself and those around you and, above all, put pleasure, taste and imagination at the top of every ingredient list you make.

La femme française

As for her identity, sadly perhaps, being everyone precludes her being anyone. To paraphrase that famous French food lover, Chaka Khan, she is every woman. There is a little part of every *femme française*, of all ages, from all parts of the country, in her. To be fair she is probably even one third male.

Should you feel the urge to personify her as you read, I suggest you pick a romantically embellished *Française* or *Français*, the one who cooked you that fabulous meal, real or fantasy, in Gordes or Biarritz or Paris or Lille all those years ago.

For there is sure to be one, because she was the forerunner. Not so long ago, about 15 years BJ (before Jamie) when taste, enjoyment and discovery were motivation enough and Elizabeth David was the only guru you needed or heeded, she was the first foreign cook you wanted to emulate.

Cooking as entertainment or as an aspirational lifestyle statement has still done little to change basic UK and Irish domestic culinary habits. Ours may be a rapidly developing food culture, but even though standards and awareness are undeniably rising, the gigantic UK food media industry (which tellingly has only a tiny French equivalent) has yet to make a real impact on the way average UK families cook on a daily basis. The proportion of ready-made or pre-assembled meals to fresh raw produce on offer in every UK supermarket is ample proof of that. There may be three types of smoked paprika there to choose from for the recipe you saw demonstrated on TV, but just how many UK or Irish people cook the way their French counterparts do?

It would seem logical then, to start looking to them for example and inspiration. In my 20 years in France with no cooking qualification other than a healthy obsession with what I eat and how I eat it, I have learned most from stallholders and other shoppers at my local market and at home cooks' tables and shoulders, not from TV, magazines, dvds or even cookery classes. Those who taught me did so unwittingly, and their most valuable knowledge was passed on unsolicited.

Food, eating and cooking are deeply infused into the French psyche. Perhaps history and geography will never allow us to achieve this level of innate love and understanding, but

now that our appetites are whetted by cooking as entertainment, we can at least approach the subject by taking a closer look at how the French cook and eat every day.

chapter 1
shops wisely

The French not only cook with passion, they shop with precision.
Despite their much-envied 35-hour week, few Frenchwomen shop for
food solely at their local market.

Today's typical weekly pattern is more likely to be a trolleyful from the
supermarket – Auchan, Carrefour or Monoprix, a leisurely weekend
market trip and two or three small top-ups at local specialist shops on
the way home from work, the school run or yoga. The majority still
queue for their daily bread, although these days the precious baguette
will often be branded Gana, Poujauran or Banette, studded with sesame

or poppy seeds or made with organic wholegrain flour. I live bang in the centre of a small town just on the edge of Paris, Saint-Germain-en-Laye, metres from a fabulously stocked Monoprix. My kitchen is so small and their opening hours so long that I treat the place as an extension of my cupboards and fridge.

food encounters

On the way to school, my children and I also pass a McDonalds, a travel agent, three banks, a pizza takeaway, two opticians, three pharmacists, five shoe shops and a Levis store, just like in Kirkcaldy, Coleraine or Kingston.

On our way home, however, we will buy the evening meal from a choice of five butcher shops, two *charcuteries*, five bakers, two *rôtisseries*, a cheese shop, a fish shop, three fruit and vegetable shops and three *traîteurs*. We will bump into school-mates, neighbours and teachers. Treats of lollipops, brioche, grapes and slivers of ham will be slipped to my kids as we wait our turn. They will usually dispute some part of the menu, but with such choice before us, a compromise is invariably found. This is the way I want them to learn about food. The way the French do. For in stark contrast to the every-man-for-himself supermarket race, buying food in small shops and at the market is a communal and convivial task.

The constant exchange of tips, experiences and recipes grows into significant, confidence-building knowledge. I often feel I am not so much buying food as entering into a mini moral contract with the seller, loath to part with his beloved produce until he is assured that I will serve it properly.

Thrown into proximity as we queue, obliged to speak up, choose and order, we suddenly become party to almost intimate details of strangers' lives.

'How many guests for the roast beef?'

'Is the cod fillet for your children? Wouldn't you prefer something without bones?'

'Is the Mont d'Or for a plateau? Would you like me to take the rind off?'

'Is the melon being eaten tonight or tomorrow?'

At weekends, the pace changes. My market is 100 metres away and if I have had a chance to shop on Friday morning, over the weekend I will have made more cooked vegetable dishes, gratins, ratatouille, soups.

But nothing is more pleasurable than Sunday morning market. At 9am it is empty and my household usually still fast asleep. It feels like I'm stealing time from the rest of the day. The stallholders are relaxed and eager, their stalls overflowing. The cafés have already been open for hours and, best of all, so has the *tabac* for the weekend papers from home. I make up my menu as I go through the aisles, allowing the seasons' smells and colours to guide me. I will find something to roast, some-thing to make a pudding from, fresh fruit and cheese for Sunday lunch. Eggs and cold meat will be for kids' tea and virtuous packed lunches to start the week and, as a Sunday treat, croissants, brioches and *pain au chocolat* for the laziest of breakfasts.

Meat and poultry

The food scares of recent years and a growing awareness of health issues have slowed France's meat consumption, but the country is still high on the list of European meat eaters. Although supermarket shopping is on the increase, and there is great concern for the future of town-centre individual food shops, a defensive government strategy has kept the *grandes surfaces* away from the hubs of even larger towns, and the majority of French shoppers still make weekly visits to the *boucherie*, *volailler* (poultry specialist) or *charcuterie*.

A French cook expects the cuts she buys to be perfectly prepared for the dish she has in mind. At the butcher's, steaks will be cut from fillets or ribs to the exact requested thickness, shoulders of lamb will be boned and rolled, or cut into chunks for a tagine, while you wait (or while you go off and find some prunes and apricots). Small slivers will be sliced from slabs of calf's liver, and steak will be transformed into as many or as few grams of mince as you desire.

Once you have bonded with your *boucher* – by showing an interest, complimenting him on what was good, or (a faster way of earning respect in France) suggesting politely and accurately how it could have been better – nothing is too much trouble for him. In many towns, competition from other shops is fierce. Butchers know that the lower prices and easy parking of the supermarkets are tempting, and that service is often what tips the scales more than a few extra grams of *steak haché* added to your order. French meat sellers are intensely proud of their produce and skill. In good butchers' shops, the certificates describing the animals' origins (often alongside plaques and medals they may have won at shows) were already proudly on display before the BSE crisis made it obligatory. Eating well is so important to the French that they trust their butchers to deliver the quality they expect.

French cattle herds are small, be they for meat or dairy: on average thirty head and rarely exceeding a hundred. Normandy and Charolais cattle breeds are the most familiar, with the hefty Aubrac and Salers from the Massif Central most prized for their beef. Reviving rarer breeds, such as the Bleue du Nord and the Rouge Flamande, used for both their milk and meat, is becoming more common, as awareness and demand for sustainable agriculture, regional specialities and higher quality take hold and the already excellent food-producing environment becomes more eco-friendly.

All is not one hundred per cent rosy in France, of course. The country has its fair share of poor standards and concerns about intensive farming of all foodstuffs, but somehow, through a mixture of playing ostrich and a quiet confidence in the majority of meat producers, food safety and quality are taken for granted. Perhaps because the French buy in specialised shops, purchasing is linked to a human face and not to supermarket aisles. BSE was famously swept under the carpet for years as the French simultaneously and vociferously banned British beef, moralistically wagging their fingers. Avian flu caused a strong dip in poultry sales but the government and food lobbies swung into action, eating chicken at every photo opportunity, and consumption is almost back to normal.

Previous pages: The displays in meat shops are as pretty and enticing as any pâtisserie and include the gastronomic wonder poulet de Bresse AOC (bottom centre) and the magnificent côte de boeuf (bottom right). The variety, abundance and careful preparation make both raw cuts and semi-ready plats traiteur seem so irresistible.

Opposite: Chicken and meat roasting at a market rôtisserie.

In this climate of confidence, as real or illusory as it may be, demand for organic meat and other organic foods has not taken off in the way it has in the UK. The French complain that the criteria for obtaining the symbol are more stringent than in other EU countries, pricing the products out of the market. Organic meat production accounts for only one per cent of the total, with supermarket chain Auchan commercialising two thirds of this. There is little or no demand for even free-range pork, let alone organic, although interest in the breeds reared is growing, with the main foodie magazines running glamorous photo features about piggy celebrity breeds such as the *cul noir*, a black-bottomed breed famous for its delicate ham. For beef and lamb, our French cook will want to know the country of origin, and avoiding anything from outside the country is already a gauge of quality (with the exception of Angus beef!) for many patriots.

Veal production is the only area where animal welfare issues have come to public prominence. There has been a large increase in awareness of poor husbandry, and as soft white calf meat becomes more and more associated with cruelty, the French are turning to *veau elevé sous la mère*, calves raised with their mother, who live part of their lives outside, grazing. This gives a pinker, stronger-tasting meat and ensures

ethical farming methods. Veal crates will be banned in France, as in the rest of Europe, in 2007. They were banned 15 years ago in the UK.

The best *charcuterie* in Saint-Germain-en-Laye, my town, is to be had at the main market. Reflecting France's impressive pork-consumption rate, there are no fewer than four stalls selling raw, cooked and preserved versions of every scrap of meat, skin and bone found on a pig: from the neat chops and rolled fillet or loins to salted knuckle and shoulder used for the slow-cooked *potées*, through the dozens of cooked pâtés, rillettes, hams, bellies, ears, snouts and trotters.

France is the fourth-largest poultry producer in the world, and the majority of its chicken is intensively farmed. There are dubious methods used just as there are in the UK, but even a lowly *poulet ordinaire* will not collapse into a bland, white spongy heap as its UK equivalent does. In French supermarkets there is usually a choice of *poulet fermier*, *bio* (organic) and *label rouge*. Both the latter are reared from hardy, rustic breeds, for a minimum of 81 days in outside enclosures with no more than 10 birds per square metre, fed on traceable vegetal feed. *Poulet fermier* spends its life outside. At the market I can choose a chicken that has lived a happy life. Poultry sellers there can often show me photos and

always tell me stories of how it was reared. A free-range, market-bought *poulet fermier* will look a bit straggly, will have its legs and head attached and its giblets inside, and when cooked will be firm, juicy and delicious. My poultry butcher will behead and defoot it, cut or truss it up just as I desire, for the barbecue, casserole or roasting tin. If I want further reassurance of quality and flavour, there is also an ultimate AOC chicken (see page 18 and caption), the *poulet de Bresse*.

In Saint-Germain-en-Laye, I buy much of my poultry at the splendid shop of Monsieur Janinet. He is the exception confirming the rule about French food shopkeepers: a quiet, grumpy man, pretty loath to discuss what he sells and where it comes from, probably deeming, with some justification, that his products' appearance and presentation speak for themselves. His specialised business certainly enjoys a monopoly in the town. A listed building, this old *rôtisserie* has sawdust on the stone floor and is bedecked in beautiful tiles set around a huge copper-fronted fireplace, in which the meat would have been roasted in the old days. In each window are two massive trophies, one a magnificent red deer stag, the other a gigantic tusked wild boar, whose dour expressions obviously provide daily inspiration to Monsieur Janinet, his wife (at the till) and his staff.

Here I will always have a choice of three or four breeds of chicken, all *label rouge* or *fermier*. As a matter of course there will be farmed poussin, quail, guinea fowl and duck. At Christmas there will also be *poularde*, turkey, capon and goose, and during the shooting season grouse, pheasant, mallard and woodcock. Like the chickens they are presented whole, their neck feathers and shiny claws making an extraordinary display on the shelves and in the shop window. Monsieur Janinet also sells foie gras, confit de canard, pork, rabbit, baby goat, lamb and game, and will grumpily take an order for anything not in stock when you require it. I remember once ordering from him thirty quail for a large dinner party without receiving so much as a thank you for my custom. They tasted fantastic.

During the shooting season, venison (from both red and roe deer), baby and adult boar and hare will all be available ready to be cooked, in long fillet roasts, or cut into pieces or chunks, marinated or not. Whole hares hang next to whole pheasants and whole skinned piglets on ancient metal hooks strung up high in the window. Outside in the courtyard, which opens onto the main shopping street, chickens, piglets, quail and ducks are roasted (with onions, garlic and herbs) over a vertical gas-powered spit, and as you breathe in you could easily imagine yourself in a medieval hunting banquet.

Quiche aux noisettes, Mont d'Or et viande des grisons

Hazelnut, mont d'or and cured beef quiche

This recipe is derived from the consensual quiche lorraine, pleasing to adults and children alike and completely free of pesky serving temperature rules (although still warm and quivering from the oven would be my preference).

In France you can vary the cheese–ham combo to your heart's delight – here I've swapped the ham for dried Swiss beef. This brings a slight Alpine touch to it, I think, and is the sort of thing I might serve to a skiing party, should anyone ever imprison me in a chalet halfway up a mountain again. And the hazelnuts in the slightly sweet pastry make the whole thing a wee bit more interesting.

I'm not saying French cooks would make this pastry every time. Or indeed even a plain version, since in even the most basic French supermarket there always seems to be a choice of very honourable sweet or savoury *brisée* (shortcrust) or *feuillétée* (puff) ready-rolled pastry, neatly attached to its own baking sheet.

I could nod to UK fashion and call this a 'tarte' – quiches seem so passé now. But one of the wonderful things about great French dishes is that they don't go out of fashion... in France. There is always a place for them on someone's table. Or in the quiche's case, in every *boulangerie* or *traiteur*.

FOR 6

2 eggs, plus 1 egg yolk
30 ml crème fraîche or double cream
**3–4 medium slices *viande de grisons*
 (or any good dried beef)**
**3–4 slices mont d'or cheese (or
 camembert, tome, or anything
 creamy and not too powerful)**
Freshly ground black pepper

FOR THE PASTRY
240 g plain flour
1^1/$_2$ tablespoons icing sugar
120 g very cold butter, diced
50 g dry-roasted hazelnuts, chopped

To make the pastry, put the flour, sugar and butter in a food-processor and whizz until the mixture resembles fine breadcrumbs. Add the hazelnuts and bind into a dough by mixing in a few teaspoonfuls of very cold water. Roll into a ball and chill for an hour or so in the fridge.

Roll out the dough and use it to line a 22 cm quiche tin (there will be more pastry than you need, to make rolling easier), then chill in the fridge again for 30 minutes if possible.

Meanwhile, preheat the oven to 180°C/350°F/gas mark 4.

Lightly beat the eggs and the extra yolk with the cream, and add some pepper. Pour the mixture into the pastry shell, place the beef and cheese slices on the top and bake for about 30 minutes until nicely golden.

Remove from the oven and forget about it until your guests arrive. Serve with fresh salad leaves.

Pintadeau rôti aux poivrons braisés

Roast guinea fowl with braised peppers

Guinea fowl has a gamey taste that stands up well to highly flavoured accompaniments. This is a tremendously easy recipe. The guinea fowl can be replaced by chicken or poussin.

FOR 6

1 guinea fowl, around 1.5 kg

2 garlic cloves, crushed

Juice and large strips of zest of
　1 orange

Olive oil

4 peppers, a mix of colours, deseeded
　and cut into strips

1 onion, sliced

6 preserved piquillo peppers, roughly
　chopped

A good handful of black olives

Salt and freshly ground black pepper

Preheat the oven to 190°C/375°F/gas mark 5.

Rub the guinea fowl all over with one of the garlic cloves and half the orange zest, then put them inside the bird. Spread some olive oil over its skin and lightly season with salt.

Cook the bird for around 1 hour 15 minutes, until the juices run clear, basting as often as you can remember. Remove from the oven and let it stand for a good 10–15 minutes before carving.

While the bird is resting, heat some olive oil in a frying pan and fry the peppers with the remaining garlic and the onion. Pour in the orange juice and stir to deglaze, add the remaining orange zest, the piquillo peppers and the olives. Heat it all through for a few minutes.

Carve the guinea fowl and serve with the seasoned peppers and olives.

Travers d'agneau façon méchoui

Lamb spare ribs with méchoui flavours

Le méchoui, or *kharouf machwi* in Arabic, is a traditional North African way of slowly roasting a small animal (goat, sheep or lamb), flavoured with spices and basted constantly, over a wood fire on an open spit. It is a popular way of feeding the multitudes at large French summer gatherings. This is my quick-fix version.

FOR 4–5

2 teaspoons cumin seeds

2 teaspoons coriander seeds

3 garlic cloves, peeled

2–3 tablespoons olive oil

2 tablespoons lemon juice

Pinch of saffron strands, optional

Harissa paste, to taste

Salt

1 kg of lamb ribs

Grind together all the ingredients except for the lamb ribs, using a pestle and mortar or in a mini food-processor. Smear the paste all over the lamb and leave it to absorb the flavours for an hour or so.

Heat the grill of your oven to hot or set up your barbecue, and cook the meat for 20–30 minutes, turning it regularly.

Serve with fresh salad vegetables or taboulé (see page 156).

Porc cuit dans du lait, romarin et sauge

Pork cooked in milk with rosemary and sage

This is a popular way of making tasty and tender pork or rabbit. It will look very curdled when just cooked, which is why I thicken the sauce at the end, but you don't have to.

FOR 6
30 g butter

2 tablespoons olive oil

1.5 kg roast of pork cut in the fillet

2 medium onions, finely chopped, plus 1 small onion studded with 2–3 cloves

1 carrot, chopped

1.5 litres full-fat milk

3 fresh sage leaves

Sprig of rosemary

1 bay leaf, fresh if possible

Pinch each of ground cinnamon and ground nutmeg

Salt and freshly ground black pepper

FOR THE SAUCE

50 g butter

1 tablespoon plain flour

In a heavy-based casserole dish with a lid, heat the butter and oil and add the pork, the chopped onions and carrot, then cook, stirring often, until the meat has browned on all sides.

Add the milk, the clove-studded onion, herbs, a little salt and pepper and the ground spices and bring to the boil. Cover and simmer very gently on a low heat for 1 hour 30 minutes – 2 hours; alternatively, transfer the dish to an oven preheated to 150°C/300°F/gas mark 2 and cook for the same length of time.

Remove the pork from the dish and keep it warm while you make the sauce.

Strain the cooking liquid through a fine sieve, then pour it into another saucepan and reduce it by letting it simmer for 5–10 minutes.

Meanwhile, make a *beurre manié* by cooking the butter with the flour for a few minutes. Pour in the reduced cooking liquid, stirring all the time. Bring to the boil, then reduce the heat and cook very gently for 1–2 minutes. Season to taste and serve with the pork.

Foie gras frais poêlé, figues trop mûres

Pan-fried foie gras with overripe figs

The best way to cook and serve foie gras at home is as simply as possible. For foie gras (fattened goose or duck's liver), that means serving it raw, seared or *mi-cuit* in a simple terrine. Texture is as much a part of the experience as taste, and when you have taken the trouble to source a good (and therefore as ethically produced as is possible) foie gras, these cooking methods will make the most of that quality.

Most serious French home cooks pride themselves on making their own *terrine de foie gras*, especially in the south-west where its production is so intertwined with everyday life. My French friends make their own terrines from recipes that use a variety of ingenious methods, from the microwave to the bain-marie, salt-crust to tea-towel, clingfilm to sterilising pots. As yet I haven't mastered my own and lazily prefer to count on my *volailler's* (poultry specialist) choice of supplier.

Pan-frying is the fastest, easiest cooking method, if smoky and fat-spitting and requiring precise preparation and timing. It allows you to play around with accompaniments, cutting through the richness of the liver with tart fruit or tangy vinegar glazes, riding along with it in the company of smooth earthy mushrooms, or contrasting the texture with the sweet crunch of toasted spiced or malted bread.

FOR 8 (see photograph on page 29)

1 whole, raw goose or duck foie gras, about 550–600g, well chilled in the fridge
8–10 slices of good malted bread, such as Poilâne or Veda
Fleur de sel (sea salt)
Freshly ground white pepper
8 overripe figs, quartered

Make sure your guests are seated, ready to eat, preferably with a glass of chilled Loupiac, Sauternes, Baumes de Venise or Condrieu in hand.

Cut the well-chilled foie gras into 1cm slices (Hugh 'Fearlessly Eatsitall' says to freeze it before slicing so that it keeps its shape, but I find that freezing makes it counterproductively mushy), avoiding and removing nerves as you go.

Have your guests' warmed plates to hand, some freshly prepared toasted bread and a large dish with lots of kitchen paper just by the hob.

Heat a frying pan until it is medium hot – no fat required, of course. Check the heat by dropping in a tiny morsel of foie gras: it should fizz and frazzle instantly. Remove it and wipe the pan clean with kitchen paper before bringing it back to the heat.

Cover as much of your stainable self as possible with something non-stainable, and quickly lay the slices of foie gras in the pan. Let them sizzle for about 1 minute, having a peek underneath after about 45 seconds. A thin, dark, caramelised crust should have formed. Flip them over very carefully (you could drain off excess fat at this stage) and cook for a further 1 minute on the other side.

Set the slices on kitchen paper for a few seconds to absorb any excess fat from the surface and transfer them to the serving plates. Sprinkle with some fleur de sel (indispensable for its less-salty-than-salt taste and crunch) and pepper, and serve with the toasted bread and figs.

gastronomiquement incorrect foie gras

Despite the development of more anti-French than pro-animal welfare pockets of resistance, foie gras has crept its way onto menus everywhere. In France, consumption has doubled over the past ten years. Foie gras is no longer eaten solely at Christmas or at grand occasions, and recipes have evolved dramatically from the traditional poached terrine (with or without truffles), as more and more home cooks buy it raw and serve it roasted or pan-fried, or built into more elaborate dishes and daringly teamed with meat, fish or shellfish.

For the first 20 years of French life, I was happy to toe the Gallic line, glibly fudging the force-feeding debate. More recently, due to growing demand within and without France, it has become difficult to find good-quality raw livers. Even those specially ordered from my *charcutier* would fizz away to nothing in the pan, giving up litres of watery fat and smoking out my kitchen.

So one Sunday I set out to a local farm's *portes ouvertes* (open door) to see if its foie gras would make the grade and find out just how ashamed of myself I should feel about eating it.

It was a beautiful day, the Ferme du Loup Ravissant (Farm of the Ravishing Wolf) being a series of charming stone buildings with a large lawn and pear tree, fields full of very attractive ducks and only a few ominous camp-like blocks visible in the distance.

As we neared the pretty fields for the start of the guided tour, I saw that the ducks were flapping like hell but seemed too heavy to take off and were not making any noise. In answer to my questions, the farmer explained that these were *mulard* ducks, sterile crosses between two breeds which, apart from not allowing feathery sex to interfere with their primary function in life, feeding us, also presented the 'great advantage' of not quacking.

Then followed a surreal, euphemism-filled tour of the 'laboratory'. We were given descriptions of how the ducks were 'bled' from inside their throats to ensure better hygiene and that the livers, unlike beef which should be hung after 'the end of living' needed to be taken out as soon as possible to make sure those nasty enzymes didn't spoil them.

Next up was the *gavage*, the force-feeding and the root of all controversy. We entered the long, dark hut where 200 death row ducks, only three days before the end of living, were standing or sitting in cages big enough to let them move around and flap their wings. They were all panting gently, beaks apart, as after

11 days of *gavage* their livers had swollen so much their lungs were starting to be compressed. A bit like being nine months pregnant, said our guide. Quite. Apart from that, they looked as happy as dumb, flightless, condemned, eunuch ducks can, I suppose.

Then, still chatting, the farmer took hold of the nearest beak, inserted a plastic tube, and released 600g of soaked corn nibs straight into the duck's tummy, gently stroking the bird's gullet to make it go down more easily. When he had finished, the duck sat down and that was that. It certainly did not look distressed, in pain, or even ruffled. Resigned (and full up) would be the words to describe any emotion or reaction showing on that ducky face.

Back at the farm kitchen, the farmer's mother gave everyone tiny pieces of 160-euro-per-kilo terrine. I was keen to taste the justification for what I had just witnessed. The terrine, the *rillettes à l'échalote*, the *saucisson* and the *magrets* were superb.

As we ate, I thought of the farmer telling us how large his cages were compared to some, how he had installed air-conditioning this summer as the ducks couldn't move enough to keep cool. How he gradually increased quantities from the start of the *gavage* to allow the ducks' digestion to grow accustomed to the home-grown corn. How the swelling of the livers was a natural phenomenon in migratory ducks and geese, not a disease, and how they would go back to normal in a week if they were returned to the fields. How he missed his geese (modern tastes have veered to a more pronounced duck flavour), as they had real character, and how his wife would feed them by hand, lovingly coaxing the corn down grain by grain.

But this is not the case with a majority of foie gras producers, especially those outside France, and one must be extremely careful to check sources, at least to ensure the quality of the foie gras, which will suffer along with the ducks or geese.

Cheese and dairy

In a famous interview with *Newsweek* in 1961, President Charles de Gaulle asked, 'How can anyone govern a country that has 246 kinds of cheese?' What he meant was 'How can anyone be expected to govern 246 different kinds of French?'

But 246 varieties of cheese was a conservative estimate, the amount is calculated to be well over 500 today.

The most distinguished cheeses are AOC (*Apellation d'Origine Controllée*, controlled designation of origin). The stringent rules for inclusion in this exclusive club are based on the product originating from a specific area in France and being produced in a traditional way. Although the AOC code is most often applied to wine production, it encompasses many food categories. After wine, the largest category is cheese and dairy, with 47 varieties of cheese, butter and cream awarded the prestigious label. Spicy, powerful roquefort is the oldest AOC, with a decree from the Toulouse parliament establishing its identity in 1666. Springy, sweet, nutty, caramel-flavoured beaufort, also known as 'the prince of gruyères' is one of the ancient Savoie region of cheeses. The creamy suppleness and mushroomy undertones of camembert and brie are known and loved the world over and stand alongside lesser-known AOCs such as *époisses*, described eloquently in a professional cheesetaster's notes as 'uncompromisingly pungent, gloriously sticky and brackish with an abundant fruity fizz.'

The 'French Paradox' is famous – how do the French manage to have half the heart disease and obesity of the British, along with the lowest average body weight per capita in the Western world, while eating such high-cholesterol food?

Attempts at explaining this paradox have always included stories of how the French savour the taste of their cheese, butter and cream, how they prolong and appreciate the pleasure these products bring them, and how they eat just a little of each cheese slowly but intensely. They will team cheese carefully with the right bread, the right butter, the right wine, religiously giving it a whole course to itself, regardless of what is coming before or after.

It is a reflex driven by an epicurean, hedonistic trait – perhaps the national characteristic I love most, appearing in many aspects of eating, and therefore, life. To my mind, it shows perfectly how French eating habits differ from ours and, yes, in this way at least, how they are better than ours. I don't know if the British as a nation can ever acquire such a deep capacity to feel that much pleasure then doggedly protect everything it takes to produce it.

A Sunday-morning visit to Maître Affineur, Sébastien Dubois's cheese temple in Saint-Germain-en-Laye will further prove the point. I wish you could see it, for instance in July when the full summer collection of goat's cheeses (his speciality) is on display, or in May, before the heat makes Sébastien put away much of the full-bodied mature stock. And do come with at least 20 euros to spend. Good cheese is expensive.

Previous pages, clockwise from top left: Ingredients for a Fontainebleau (see also recipe on page 40): cream and fromage frais. M. Dubois's cheese shop. Retro glass pots for yogurt. Fresh eggs at the market. Goat's cheeses from Maître Affineur. Cheese at the market in Arles.
Opposite: Baked camembert (see also recipe on page 35).

The *fromagerie* is housed in a splendid, purpose-built building constructed in 1897. It is all swathed in marble and oak, with cellars beneath. On Sunday, Sébastien will be there himself, moustachioed, of course, appropriately rotund, with two trusty salesmen at his shoulders. The customers will come in slowly, pulling their clothes around them in the cool atmosphere, excited yet quietly determined. They will examine the cheeses sitting naked all around them, uncovered by glass or plastic of any sort, as if they were jewels or exhibits in a museum. You can see people concentrating, visualising and building their Sunday *plateau de fromages* as they move about the shop: first, a good blue, a roquefort, or a bleu d'Auvergne, so potent it will have its own knife on the cheeseboard; then something full-bodied and creamy, like a brie de meaux, or a reblochon, or a chaource; then one with a bit of punch like a mature munster or a good old comté. They might add something dry, an old chavignol would do, or a cracked orange mimolette; and finally, a little *douceur* (sweetness), a gently moist, tangy and crumbling fresh goat's cheese, perhaps a valençay or an ashy slice of cendré. Instructions are given and Sébastien cuts tiny slivers and chunks, wrapping each piece as he goes, no matter how long the queue behind.

Reading the goat's cheese names chez Sébastien is like reading an aristocratic guest list from the ball in Flaubert's Madame Bovary: Bonde de Sologne, Capri des Deux Sèvres, Tricorne de Jonsac, Tominette de la Dalmerie, Pérail des Cabasses... Imaginatively evocative of their shapes are *perle* (pearl) *des Cevennes*, *feuille* (leaf) *du Limousin*, *figuette* (little fig) *du Tarn* and my favourite, *la taupinette* (little molehill) *des Charentes*. Sébastien also magnanimously stocks stilton and cheddar, the only two UK cheeses he reckons are worth their perch beside other exotic items such as Spanish manchego and Italian pecorino.

If you can get him talking in a quiet moment, Sébastien will explain how he chooses his suppliers. All the cheese, cream, milk and butter he sells come from small farms and dairies where the milk is collected and transformed every day, not anonymously sent off to industrial dairies and stocked for days before becoming cheese, butter or cream. He will speak of his love of his trade and *affinage* (how he ripens and matures the cheese in the cellars beneath the shop). I'm dying for an invitation to explore them with him, but I dare not ask. I'm slowly getting used to jealous secrecy among French food craftsmen. And after all, I am in France. This is a mini factory and his livelihood. It is not a tourist attraction.

Brie truffé

Ripe truffled brie

It's amazing how two such smelly items go so well together, but they do. This recipe was given to me by Véronique, *cuisinière extraordinaire* who always has a truffle or two stashed in her kitchen throughout the winter. It's a great way of getting a little truffle to go a long way, and an impressive cheese course to serve for a large gathering.

FOR 4 (multiply up according to the
number of guests and the size of the brie)
20 g black truffle, as fresh as possible
2 tablespoons mascarpone cheese
400 g 'ripe' brie, such as brie de meaux
or brie de melun (photo)
Fleur de sel (sea salt)

Grate the truffle into the mascarpone and mix well.

Slice the brie in two horizontally, and spread the truffle cream on one half as you would do with a sandwich. Put the other half on top and press down lightly.

Wrap the cheese up tightly in clingfilm and leave it in the fridge for a day to let the truffle flavour permeate throughout the cheese.

Allow the cheese to come to room temperature before serving with some really good bread.

Œufs à la coque, mouillettes aux truffes

Soft-boiled eggs with truffle butter eggy soldiers

A great way to eat truffles. Simple and decadent.

FOR 2

15g black truffle, as fresh as possible

80g best-quality salted butter, softened

2 eggs

4 slices of good white bread

Grate the truffle into the softened butter, mix well, cover and leave for at least an hour to let the flavours mingle.

Soft-boil the eggs, toast the bread, spread with the butter and cut into fingers for dipping into the runny egg yolk.

Brocciu Corse au miel Corsican brocciu with honey

Brocciu is the most famous Corsican cheese, made from unpasteurised goat's or sheep's milk and, when young, is similar to Italian ricotta. Eaten fresh with jam or honey it can be the cheese course or dessert. If you can find some, Corsican woodland honey (*miel du maquis Corse*) is perfect here, of course.

FOR 4

1 brocciu cheese (about 200g), well chilled and removed from its mould

4–5 tablespoons good honey

Cut the cheese into slices and drizzle with honey. Serve with crusty *pain de campagne*.

Camembert rôti dans sa boîte

Camembert baked in its box

An easy way to jazz up the cheese course. Or serve it as a starter.

FOR 6 (see photograph on page 33)

1 ripe camembert in its wooden box

Endives, celery, apples and baguette for dipping and scooping

Preheat the oven to 180°C/350°F/gas mark 4.

Remove the paper covering from the cheese and bake for about 10 minutes or until the cheese feels molten beneath the crust.

Peel back the top crust and serve immediately.

Beurre de crevettes grises, pain Poilâne

Prawn butter on toasted Poilâne bread

FOR 4–6

200 g shelled grey prawns, fresh
   if possible
200 g salted butter, softened
4–6 slices of Poilâne malted bread
Ground white pepper

Lionel Poilâne was a star, a famous Parisian baker who died tragically in a helicopter accident. His genius, moist and malty bread, lives on through his shops now managed by his daughter.

Reserve a few prawns for garnish. In a food-processor, whizz the rest of the prawns with the butter and some pepper. Chill in the fridge so the butter hardens again. Serve it with the toasted Poilâne.

Ravioli de betteraves et Comté aux poires

Beetroot and comté ravioli with pears

Sometimes the way French restaurants puff up their menus can be very irritating. Even with a good level of French it is difficult enough translating the ingredients themselves, let alone interpreting just what might be on your plate in a little nest of this or a farandole of that.

When I cook formal meals, I often apply what I have learned from confident French hosts by writing out the 'menu' for my guests. The aim is to, hopefully, heighten their anticipation and allow them to pace themselves through the meal. For the host, menus are also useful as an *aide-mémoire* if you have had a glass of wine too many or get too enthralled with the conversation.

Here is a little restaurant-menu teasing which, admittedly, borders on pretension. Of course these ravioli are not made from pasta. The beetroot is simply the top and bottom layer of a large open 'ravioli', with comté cheese and pear in between.

FOR 4

400 g mature comté cheese, cut into
   1 cm cubes
2 large cooked beetroots, thinly sliced
1 ripe pear, peeled and finely diced
1 dried pear, finely diced
2–3 tablespoons gentle olive oil
Squeeze of lemon juice
$1/2$ preserved lemon, finely diced
Flat-leaf parsley, to garnish
Salt and freshly ground black pepper

Construct very loose 'ravioli' by placing some comté chunks on a slice of beetroot and laying a second beetroot slice loosely over the top.

In a bowl, combine the ripe and dried pears, olive oil, lemon juice and preserved lemon. Season and mix well. Spoon the mixture over the 'ravioli', garnish with sprigs of flat-leaf parsley and serve immediately.

Quatre-quarts à la fleur de sel, compote de rhubarbe et fraises

Salted butter cake with rhubarb and strawberry compote

This is the classic French all-in-one butter sponge or pound cake, called *quatre-quarts*, or four quarters, as its four main ingredients are all the same weight. Flavoured with chocolate, lemon zest or vanilla, it's the perfect Sunday afternoon cake.

I always like to make it with salted butter. This might be more from nostalgia for salty Irish Dromona, used in both the sponge and the icing on the cakes of my childhood, than any culinary justification. Either way, both nostalgia and culinary requirements get satisfied in Saint-Germain-en-Laye, thanks to a choice of lovely *fleur de sel* butter sparkling with tiny, crunchy less-salty-than-salt crystals at both the *crémerie* and supermarket.

Serious French home cooks with big enough pantries or cellars make compotes and *coulis* all summer long. Seasonal gluts fill rows of fat *bocaux* (glass jars) with enough apricots, figs, cherries and peaches to last throughout the winter.

The strawberries in this compote are only here to give some spring colour to the properly grown but often disappointingly brownish-green rhubarb I often seem to come across in Paris. Further south I'm sure it's not an issue. If you have access to pink ripeness that also tastes good, look no further: the acidic twang of the fruit will always provide a simple and satisfying contrast to the sweet, buttery cake.

Quatre-quarts

FOR 8

225 g plain flour
225 g caster sugar
225 g good-quality salted butter or fleur de sel butter, softened
1½ teaspoons baking powder
A few drops of vanilla extract
4 medium eggs, at room temperature

Preheat the oven to 180°C/350°F/gas mark 4.

Grease and flour a 22 cm, round sandwich tin or use a 'magical' silicone one.

Beat all the ingredients together in a mixer on high for 2 minutes or so, scraping the sides of the bowl halfway through. Tip the mixture into the tin and bake for 25–30 minutes, until it is beautifully golden and just coming away from the sides of the tin.

Remove from the oven, let it cool slightly then turn out onto a wire rack and leave to cool completely.

Rhubarb and strawberry compote

FOR THE COMPOTE

500 g rhubarb, cut into chunks
200 g strawberries, hulled and sliced
2–3 tablespoons caster sugar

Put the rhubarb in a pan with a tiny splash of water. Cover and heat very gently, leaving it to steam in its own juices for 10–15 minutes or until soft. If you are adding strawberries, do it now. They will poach and in so doing release their juicy dye. Add the sugar and purée the whole thing if you wish – but do you really want to have more equipment to take out, wash and put away on a Sunday afternoon?

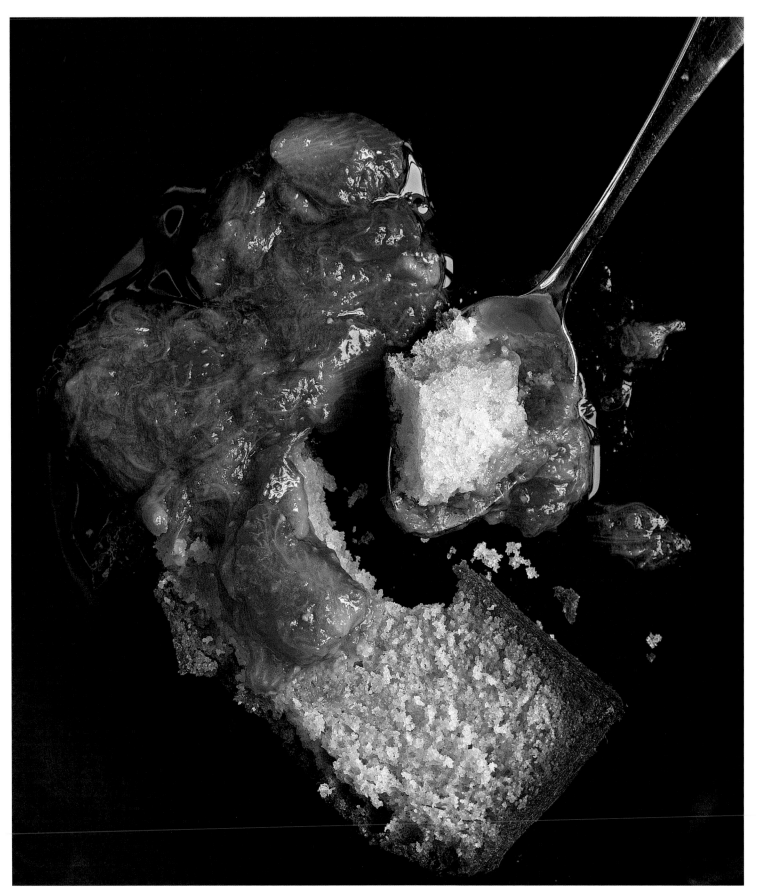

Fontainebleau au sucre vanillé

Fountainebleau with vanilla sugar

This is a retro dessert of fromage frais whipped frothy with cream, traditionally made to order in dairy shops.

FOR 4

300g fromage frais, 20 per cent fat
250ml whipping cream
30g (2 sachets) vanilla sugar

Put all the ingredients in a mixing bowl and whip briskly to form a frothy chantilly cream. Serve immediately.

Glace à la crème fraîche

'Raw' crème fraîche ice cream with lavender shortbread

With a shelf life of only six days and therefore sold only in specialist dairy shops and in markets, 'raw' or unpasteurised milk and cream have a cleaner, deeper, more floral taste than their pasteurised counterparts. You can almost taste the hay and grass and wild flowers the cows have munched. *Crème fraîche crue* is a gorgeously decadent cream. Its colour is near to that of putty, and its 40 per cent fat content makes it flow slowly and heavily off the ladle like honey. It is mesmerising standing in the queue at the market, watching the stallholder dip again and again into his huge bucket to fill the traditional white pots, which are then greedily stashed away in customers' baskets.

Cheese made with unpasteurised milk is widely available within France, and the sixty-day maturation listeria-scare rule for exports has been hugely scoffed at – although French pregnant women are advised to avoid ripe unpasteurised camembert and similar cheeses. Fantastic butter, yogurt and other products made from unpasteurised goat's and ewe's milk can also be found at the specialist dairy shops, still thankfully very numerous. However, unpasteurised milk legislation has been made extremely strict and it is now forbidden, for example, in ice-cream making, however *artisanal*.

The nearest to the 'cooked milk' taste we know in our creams, be they single, double, clotted or whipping, appears in *crème fraîche liquide* (also known as *crème fleurette fraîche*), which is fresh cream that has been flash-pasteurised for 30 seconds. It has a fat content usually between 30 and 40 per cent and is perfect for whipping and cooking. *Crème fraîche épaisse* is the same product, with the same fat content, but has been cultured and therefore thickens and takes on the distinctive tangy taste with which we have become familiar. It is fine for thickening sauces but will often curdle if cooked. Both these creams must be stored in the fridge and, if unopened, will keep there for up to 30 days. One *crème fraîche épaisse*, the fine cream from Isigny in Normandy, holds the prestigious AOC label.

UHT milk and cream have a distinctive caramel undertone and gooey texture and keep unrefrigerated for up to four months. I am still amazed at how many children in France are reared on this awful stuff. It seems paradoxical in such a cheese- and cream-loving country. Mine are lucky enough to have a mother who as a child had fresh milk awaiting her every morning, sometimes frozen, sometimes checked out by the blue tits, and who sees no problem in lugging from the shop the two fresh litres they drink every day. With their baguette-loving genes just as developed as my UHT-hating ones, my sons have no objections to nipping out to the bakers for bread at 7.30am before school. With the raspberry jam I make in the summer from County Fife raspberries, 'raw-milk' salted butter from Normandy, fresh milk *chocolat chaud* and fluffy baguette, our breakfasts really are the best of both worlds.

Lavender shortbread

100 g caster sugar
125 g butter
1 egg
2 teaspoons lavender flowers
150 g self-raising flour

Preheat the oven to 160°C/325°F/gas mark 3.

Put the sugar in a bowl. Cut the butter into small pieces and add it to the sugar. Cream them together using hand-held electric beaters, add the egg and beat well again with the beaters.

Once it is all well mixed, gently stir in the lavender flowers and then fold in the flour. Mix lightly until all the flour has been incorporated into the creamed mixture.

Use a teaspoon to spoon out onto a greased baking tray or a silicone baking mat, leaving plenty of room between each to allow for spreading during cooking. Bake for 15 minutes, then turn out onto wire racks to cool.

Crème fraîche ice cream

750 ml double cream
1 vanilla pod, split lengthways
12 medium egg yolks
150 g sugar, caster or granulated
400 ml *crème fraîche épaisse*, unpasteurised if you can get it

Put the double cream in a saucepan, add the vanilla and heat to boiling point. Meanwhile, use an electric beater to beat the egg yolks and the sugar together until they are pale and fluffy and have doubled in volume.

Pour the hot cream onto the egg mixture, stirring vigorously, then transfer the custard back into the pan and return it to a medium heat. Stirring continuously with a wooden spoon, heat the custard. When it thickens enough for your finger to leave a distinct trace on the back of the wooden spoon, remove it from the stove and pour it immediately into a large, cool bowl to prevent it from cooking in its residual heat.

Let it cool slightly, then mix in the crème fraîche. Leave to cool completely before putting it into an ice-cream maker.

Fish and shellfish

A good French fish shop or market stall is a wonder to behold. Laid out in an intricate mosaic, heads overlapping tails, are often 20 types of fish, their sandy, silver-pink or silver-blue skin gleaming against pristine white ice chips, surrounded by shellfish (*fruits de mer* or fruit of the sea). You can smell that sea. There will be three or four types and sizes of oyster (more around Christmas), all available to taste there and then, to help you choose between the salty *pleine mer*, the *fines de clairs* or the nutty, delicate *bellons*.

Heaped on ice or in wicker baskets studded with bits of seaweed will be shiny purple mussels, copper-tinged sea urchins, winkles, cockles, razors, whelks, craggy 'sea snails' in the south, stocky crayfish and lanky, flamingo-pink langoustines. Lemon and parsley will be popped as a gift into the bag along with whatever you have bought. At the *traiteur* counter, you can find home-made (*fait maison*) terrines, brandade, mayonnaises, sauce tartare, sauce verte, capers, marinated anchovies, smoked salmon, salt cod, taramasalata and fish roe.

If you buy your fish whole, according to the species and the size of fish, the fishmonger will ask, '*Vidé? Ecaillé? En filet? En entier? Avec la tête?*', and will then gut, descale, fillet, skin, behead and betail just about anything at record speed (drawing the line at sardines!). If you so wish, leftover bits will be wrapped separately for *fumet* (fish stock). Many of the fish will also be on offer ready-filleted. If the fishmonger knows children will be eating some, he will give you the *special enfants*, pieces that are guaranteed to be boneless.

But the most magical thing the fishmonger can do for you, sometimes with just a few hours' notice, but usually *sur commande* the day before, is to make up a *plateau de fruits de mer*, a shellfish platter. A bespoke collection assembled according to your budget, it will feature the like of cooked *tourteaux* (a type of crab) lobster or spider crab, ready-opened oysters, winkles, prawns and langoustines. They will be presented with pride and flair on a large ice-lined platter, wrapped up in fancy cellophane like a Christmas present. Just pick it up and the meal is ready, for with a *plateau* you usually forgo starters as it takes so long to dissect the beasts and poke out all those lovely, rich and surprisingly filling morsels. All you have to do is find some good malty bread (*pain de seigle*) and some salt-crystal butter, make (or buy) some mayonnaise and open a bottle or two of Sancerre, or Pouilly, or a decent rosé de Provence.

I learned most about cooking and eating fish from my typically food-crazy *belle-famille* (in-laws). In my first years in France I spent many weekends in renowned fishing territory, near Honfleur and Cherbourg in Normandy, at family gatherings in which much sailing and fishing were done. They are dismally mediocre but ever-optimistic fishermen, and would argue for hours about how the tackle they bought, the bait they used, and the tide or the speed of the boat had made that big one get away again.

As a result and to my great joy, we would invariably end up in fabulous fish shops in Deauville, Honfleur or Cherbourg to buy the supper we had hoped to catch. After a discussion about the menu, which would start just after breakfast and go

Previous pages, clockwise from top left: sardines, sea snails in Arles. Breton lobster. Neatly packed fish in Arles. Little crabs for making bisque. Tellines cooked in parsley, garlic and white wine at the market in St Rémy, .
Opposite: An assortment of mini fish sold as, and for, bouillabaisse in Arles.

on all day, my father-in-law did all the choosing and most of the cooking. In winter, he would roast whole bream or sea bass stuffed with herbs and garlic over the enormous wood fire in the sitting room, and in summer cook mackerel and sardines outside on a little fired-earth barbecue he brought back in his hand luggage from the West Indies. Sometimes he would poach *roussette* in fish stock and my mother-in-law would be allowed to make a herb-flavoured cream sauce and steamed potatoes to accompany his creation. The cooked fish always came after mountains of oysters, langoustines or prawns, the latter bought live and flambéed in whisky in a blackened, long-handled cast-iron pan over the fire.

My brother-in-law inherited the family's beach house near Cherbourg, and with it their charming townie ineptitude at fishing anything but the odd undersized flatfish or crab, immediately recycled as bait for the next fruitless try. We spent many summers there during our children's bucket-and-spade years. The social life on the beach was a crushingly codified extension of Cherbourg's isolated provincial bourgeois circle, and the most fun I would have away from sandcastles and rock pools was at Cherbourg's best fish shop. It is important to realise that one of the useful things about being a foreigner buying food in France is that you are

considered faintly ridiculous just by being one, so stupid questions are expected of you. Stupid (to the fishmonger and the other French customers, but not to me) questions were therefore what I asked. Persistently. In doing so, I caught up a little with 'the knowledge' that every French woman seems to possess from birth. This would seem to corroborate the French expression, '*Le ridicule ne tue pas*' (ridicule won't kill you).

But once you become familiar to the fishmonger (or for that matter, to the butcher, or the cheese seller) and he has realised you are in France for a little longer than a two-week holiday, you must move on to flirting if you want to get the best information, recipes or produce.

I am constantly amused by how *coquine* (naughty) even the most prim and demure seventy-year-old becomes as she buys ingredients for lunch or dinner. She will feign embarrassment, then relax and smile and bask in the attention, however *osé* (daring) it may be. 'Good morning Mademoiselle, you *are* looking gorgeous this morning, on your way to a date? Have I got a tasty little something for you today…'. I remember how six very posh-looking ladies waiting to be served at my favourite fishmonger's stall fell about laughing when they were invited to touch the lobsters' 'tails' to see how 'frisky' they were. And they did.

Huîtres chaudes au champagne

Oysters grilled in a champagne sabayon

This is a wonderfully festive dish. Of course you do not need to splash out on champagne – a good white wine, or even cider, would do. But the oysters-and-champagne sauce combination feels so rich and decadent it's a shame not to go the whole way.

FOR 4

24 (2 dozen) large deep oysters, for example, *fines de clairs*
About 1kg coarse sea salt
250ml champagne
5 egg yolks
2 tablespoons double cream
Freshly ground black pepper

Open the oysters over a large bowl in order to catch the water held in their shells, and set the flesh aside. Filter the liquid to remove any fragments of shell and pour it into a saucepan.

Spread a deep layer of the sea salt on a large tray. Carefully clean the bottom half of each shell and wedge them steady into the salt.

Bring the oyster water to the boil and poach the oysters for 30 seconds, no more. Drain them, retaining the poaching liquid, then place each oyster back in a shell (it doesn't have to be the one it came from!).

Heat the grill until red hot. Bring the oyster poaching water to the boil again, add the champagne and some pepper and continue to heat the liquid at a gentle boil for about 3 minutes to reduce it. Remove the pan from the heat.

In a mixing bowl, beat the egg yolks until pale and fluffy, then pour them very slowly into the champagne mix, whisking all the time.

Put the pan back on a very gentle heat, still whisking like mad. Cook for 3 minutes, or until the mixture thickens, then take it off the heat and whisk in the double cream.

Spoon the sabayon (for that is what you have just produced) into each oyster shell and brown them under the hot grill for about 2 minutes.

Serve with chilled champagne, *bien sûr*.

Chapon braisé aux olives, tomates et fenouil

Braised chapon with olives, tomatoes and fennel

The first time I ate this dish was on summer holiday in the mid 1980s, at the beach-front restaurant of the famous Cala Rossa hotel in Corsica. It was a signature dish and I thought I was getting capon, the bird. Chapon is in fact a large fish, truly meaty but fish all the same; it also goes by the name of *rascasse*. My then future husband gallantly put me right just in time, saving me from surefire ridicule from the typically disdainful waiter if I had complained of being served the wrong dish. For in those days, one of the other million things I didn't know about French cooking was that capon, the bird, was only served at Christmas. It would have been like complaining you had been brought summer pudding instead of Christmas pudding at the Savoy in July.

I still have many things to learn about French cooking. French fish names still stump me every time. Every 100 kilometres you travel around the coast there seems to be a dozen or so new species, or at least new names, to discover. But I do know that for this recipe, if you can't get chapon, then bream or red snapper will do nicely.

FOR 4

75 ml olive oil

10 tomatoes, skinned and coarsely
chopped

1 bouquet garni

2 whole chapons, about 800 g each

1 tablespoon fennel seeds

500 ml fish stock, fresh if possible

50 g black olives, chopped

2 good handfuls basil leaves, chopped

Salt and freshly ground black pepper

Preheat the oven to 190°C/375°F/gas mark 5.

In a wide pan, heat a couple of tablespoons of the olive oil and briskly fry the tomatoes to remove much of their moisture. Season with salt and pepper, add the bouquet garni and cook gently for 20 minutes, stirring frequently.

Wash and dry the fish. Put the fennel seeds in the stomach cavity, season with salt and pepper and place the fish in a large gratin dish or clay roasting dish.

Pour the tomatoes, the fish stock and the remaining olive oil around the fish and cook in the oven for 30 minutes or so, or until the flesh lifts easily off the spine with the tip of a knife.

Remove the fish from the dish, add the chopped olives and basil to the sauce, check the seasoning and serve.

You could accompany the dish with olive and garlic mash or with sautéed courgettes and aubergines.

Rouget grillé, sauce vierge

Grilled red mullet with tomato and saffron sauce

Sauce vierge has a base of peeled diced tomatoes and shallots, with garlic, lemon juice, olive oil and fresh herbs, usually basil and flat-leaf parsley. It is often served with fish and shellfish, and is also good with steamed asparagus and courgettes. It is beautifully versatile: it can be served just-made crisp, or marinated and infused, and either cold or warm. It also allows itself alliances with spices such as vanilla, nutmeg and cinnamon. Here I've included saffron as this is the way I first tasted it, made by French friends on a boat in Antibes many moons ago.

FOR 4

8 red mullet

Olive oil, for basting

FOR THE SAUCE VIERGE

4 ripe yet firm tomatoes, skinned, deseeded and finely diced

4 small shallots, finely chopped

1 garlic clove, crushed

5 tablespoons olive oil

2 tablespoons capers

Juice of 1 lemon

A handful of basil leaves, chopped

A handful of flat-leaf parsley, chopped

Pinch of saffron strands

Salt and freshly ground black pepper

Before preparing the barbecue, combine all the sauce ingredients, give it a good stir and leave the flavours to develop while you have a glass of rosé.

Rub the fish all over with a little oil and grill on the barbecue for about 5 minutes each side.

Serve with the sauce vierge, and some good crusty bread to mop up the juices.

Daurade rose rôtie, compote de rhubarbe et oignons rouges

Roasted whole pink bream with rhubarb and red onion compote

The meaty taste and texture of the fish sits well with the robust combination of rhubarb and red onion. The colours also work beautifully.

FOR 4–6

A few tablespoons olive oil

3 red onions, sliced

3–4 medium stalks rhubarb, peeled and sliced

1 pink bream, 1.2–1.5 kg, cleaned and descaled (ask your fishmonger to do this)

1.5 kg new potatoes, scrubbed

100 g salted butter

2–3 tablespoons double cream (optional)

Fleur de sel (sea salt) and freshly ground black pepper

Prepare the compote before the meal and have the potatoes in a pan, ready to boil, at the same time as the fish goes in the oven.

To make the compote, heat a little olive oil in a heavy-based pan and add the sliced onions. Cook down very gently for 5 minutes or so (you don't want them to fry or colour). When they start to soften, add the rhubarb and a splash of water. Cover the pan and let the compote cook slowly for a further 5–10 minutes, until soft. Season with *fleur de sel* and pepper and leave to cool.

Preheat the oven to 190°C/375°F/gas mark 5.

Put the fish on a baking tray and lightly cover the skin with a little olive oil. Sprinkle with a little salt and pepper.

About 20 minutes before serving (hard to gauge, of course, but it will be the only part of the meal you need to keep an eye on) pop the fish into the oven, pour boiling water on the potatoes and cook both for 20–25 minutes. Check the fish: it is ready when the flesh comes away easily from the spine. Try to catch it when it is slightly underdone and moist.

Reheat up the compote. Drain the potatoes, top with the butter and cream and crush coarsely by hand with a fork or a masher. Season and serve immediately with the fish and compote.

Velouté de châtaignes, beurre aux coraux d'oursins

Chestnut velouté with sea urchin roe butter

This surf–turf combination contrasts sweet rich chestnuts with the smoky iodic taste of sea urchins. If fresh, have your fishmonger open them for you but make sure you use the roe promptly; urchins go off as quickly as oysters. Tinned roe avoids the little pieces of shell or spine that can give an unwanted grittiness.

FOR 4

500 ml fresh chicken or vegetable stock (or water if you don't have good stock)

300 g cooked peeled chestnuts

250 ml single cream

1 tablespoon sea urchin roe

150 g salted butter, softened

1 baguette bread

Salt and freshly ground black pepper

Bring the stock or water to the boil, then add the chestnuts and cook for about 10 minutes until very soft. Liquidise in a food-processor and add the cream. Season to taste.

Mash the roe with the butter, then pop it back in the fridge to harden again.

Toast thin slices of baguette and serve spread with the roe butter, set on the hot chestnut velouté.

gastronomiquement incorrect
sea creatures

Leviticus 11: 9–12

10 And all that have not fins and scales in the seas, and in the rivers, of all that move in the waters, and of any living thing which is in the waters, they shall be an abomination unto you:

11 They shall be even an abomination unto you; ye shall not eat of their flesh, but ye shall have their carcases in abomination.

12 Whatsoever hath no fins nor scales in the waters, that shall be an abomination unto you.

Powerful as these verses may be, luckily their effect has worn off faster in France than in the UK. Seafood is considered to be a great natural bounty, on a par with fish, fruit and mushrooms, to be rejoiced in and feasted upon. The very way it is presented, piled high on fishmongers' stalls and *plateaux de fruits de mer* in restaurants, incites you to literally dig in with fingers and teeth.

The French, as conscious of taste as of health issues, are very particular about where and how they eat their sea creatures. Oysters are avoided during months without an R in their name, in other words, during the summer breeding season when they are milky inside and stocks need to be replenished. Mussels are chosen *du bouchot*, farmed on wooden posts, thus avoiding sand and impurities, and if langoustines or grey prawns arrive so fresh from the boat that they are still alive, their price rockets and they are snapped up within minutes.

Fishmongers prepare elaborate plateaux for their customers, wrapping them as prettily as a dozen roses. The *plateaux de fruits de mer* is a supremely festive dish. It is the perfect light and vitamin-filled Christmas day lunch after the foie-gras-rich midnight *réveillon* of the 24th. Fishmongers, along with other key foodsellers, all open on Christmas morning to ensure maximum freshness.

Sometimes tasting the innards of more obscure molluscs requires a real leap of faith. This is the case with sea urchins, as you have to push aside some pretty unappetising mush to get to the delicious shiny orange 'corals'. In the south of France squidgy *violettes* should be cut open and something yellow inside is meant to taste fantastic. I have now bought them three times without having the courage to go any further.

Oysters, however, are completely addictive, building cravings as strong as for steak or chocolate for those who get hooked. Many restaurants, especially traditional *brasseries*, have their *écailler* (oyster shucker) posted on the pavement outside behind an icy counter of oysters and other seafood. His are the skilled hands which choose, open and place the shells, crabs and lobsters on the diners' plates inside. To feed the national habit, all over France in the winter months, makeshift stalls are set up on Friday and Saturday evenings with ten different sorts of oysters. You will choose between the salty *pleine mer*, the nutty flat *belon* or the refined *Marennes d'oléron* in four or five sizes. Then they will be opened before you and within minutes arranged on fresh seaweed with a half lemon. That's what I call fast food.

Rosace de St Jacques aux truffes

Rosace of scallops and truffles

With the trend for sushi, fish and shellfish find themselves arranged in elaborate forms. Here, the effect you are aiming for is alternating thin slices of blackest black (truffle) and whitest white (scallop).

If the layered *millefeuille* (the thousand layered pâtisserie) proves too difficult for your knife and construction skills, try making carpaccio (like Italian thinly sliced raw beef), or, even easier, a round overlapping rosace. But really, when these two superstars meet so simply, it's difficult to go wrong. This is the dish to serve when you want to spoil someone.

FOR 2

4 blisteringly fresh scallops, corals
   and any non-white remnant of
   coral removed
1 fresh black truffle, ideally of the
   same diameter as the scallops
A few drops of mild olive oil,
   or an aromatic oil such as hazelnut,
   or walnut or argan oil mixed with
   olive oil
Fleur de sel (sea salt)

Slice the scallops and the truffle oh-so-thinly and arrange alternating slices, piled up neatly as a *millefeuille*, flat as carpaccio or in a circle as a rosace.

Drizzle very lightly with the oil and sprinkle with *fleur de sel*.

Ecrevisses à la nage

Crayfish poached in white wine

Crayfish, little freshwater lobsters, were on the verge of extinction due to pollution in France's rivers and lakes. Now, thanks to their being farmed, they are becoming more easily available though as yet have not dethroned langoustines. Their flaming shells (in French you go red as a crayfish, not a beetroot which makes sense really) and cute looks (they have extraordinary teddy-bear eyes) made them the star of many medieval banquet centrepieces, and Marie Antoinette adored them. They are part of two classic French recipes, currently branded old-fashioned but which will no doubt make a comeback in a century or two: *quenelles de brochet à la sauce nantua* (pike dumplings with a tomato and crayfish sauce), and *poulet aux écrevisses* (chicken with crayfish). This is the simplest way of cooking them and good as an introduction to the species.

Put all the ingredients except the crayfish and salt and pepper into a large pan with 500 ml water. Bring to the boil, then reduce the heat and simmer to a stock for about 20 minutes, until the carrots are tender. Season with salt and pepper to taste.

Meanwhile, wash the crayfish thoroughly.

When the carrots are tender, add the crayfish to the boiling vegetable stock, bring back to the boil and cook for 8–10 minutes.

Remove the crayfish from the stock and serve, with the stock in bowls alongside.

FOR 6

2 carrots, sliced

2 leeks, green foliage removed, finely sliced

1 onion, finely chopped

1 small celery stick, chopped

1 bouquet garni

1 small dried medium-strength chilli (optional)

250 ml dry white wine

24–30 fresh crayfish*

Salt and freshly ground black pepper

*As with langoustines, freshness is vital. A premium is paid for live crayfish as their freshness is thus undeniable. Mostly they will be available dead, and it is important to know what to look for to avoid nasty food poisoning. Your nose is the best guide. They should not smell fishy, or of ammonia. They should have no smell at all, or just a faint, pleasant briny aroma that reminds you of the sea they should have been in only a few hours previously. If they are defrosted, they will appear more limp.

Homard Breton au beurre de vanille

Lobster in vanilla butter

A defining moment in the Frenchification of my cooking (and therefore of my life) was when my son Tanguy, then five, appeared beside me in the kitchen, horrified, just as I was lowering a frisky lobster into a huge pan of boiling water. 'What are you doing Mummy?' A wave of guilt flooded over me and I had to quickly choose between using some watery euphemism like 'Don't worry darling, he's just having a nice warm bath', or telling him the truth about why one living being can boil alive another. Well, I plumped for the latter, explaining how lobsters tasted better when they were cooked that way and how they, along with langoustines and crabs, couldn't feel pain the way we did. He seemed perfectly content with that, just as he was with Father Christmas and the Tooth Fairy and the Easter Rabbit.

When selecting lobsters, avoid those that have been kept for months in the depths of dark, ill-lit tanks in small fishmongers hundreds of miles from the sea; they will have lost taste and tone. A good way to tell whether they have spent too long in captivity is the length of their antennae: as you fold them back, they should be long enough to touch the tip of the lobsters' tails, not stunted by fights or friction in a *vivier*.

Don't be fooled by 'bigger is better', either. If a lobster weighs more than 3kg it will be very old. You should be keeping it as an exhibit, not eating it. It will have fought many briny battles and be tough as old boots. If you are treating yourself to a whole lobster, a 500–600g specimen will give maximum flavour and quality of texture. Buy them weighing up to a kilo if you are sharing. Note that I don't believe all the sexist stuff French fishmongers come out with about the females being sweeter and 'fuller' than the males, but perhaps it is worth further investigation.

FOR 4

2 lively good-sized lobsters (about 750–800 g each) or 4 of around 500g each
250g (yes, yes) salted butter
1 vanilla pod, split lengthways
Sea salt and freshly ground black pepper

Bring a pan of water large enough to contain the lobsters to a vigorous boil, and add a good pinch of sea salt and pepper – I always avoid any other flavouring in the water; lobster meat needs no tweaking.

Take the rubber bands off the lobsters' claws (be very careful, they can do a lot of damage to fingers) and put the lobsters in the water. Cover the pan and cook for 15–20 minutes until the flesh turns white and starts to come away from the shell. It is better to undercook than overcook otherwise it will dry out.

Remove the lobsters from the pan with a slotted spoon and straighten them out on a wooden board to allow them to cool.

In a small pan, melt the butter mixed with the seeds scraped from the vanilla pod and the split pod itself in order to extract even more flavour.

With a very strong, very sharp knife, cut the lobsters in half lengthways from head to tail, and serve with the vanilla butter and many, many napkins.

Fruit and vegetables

Opposite, clockwise from top left: Artichokes. Heirloom tomatoes. A garlic mountain. Butter beans. White pumpkins. Beetroot and red onions.

France's moderate climate and diverse landscape – from snow-topped mountains in the Alps through volcanic valleys in the Massif Central, lush green pastures in Normandy, arid plains in Provence and thick forests in the Basque country – have created one enormous vegetable garden and orchard. The French's dice have always been loaded when it comes to fruit and vegetables, and the way our French cook buys, cooks and serves them is still in sharp contrast to UK habits. Local markets, supermarkets and greengrocers, down to the most humble corner shop, will all have a great selection.

A July inventory of my tiny two-metre shopfront *Arabe* in Paris included turnips, leeks, celery, carrots, onions, spring onions, potatoes, courgettes, asparagus and artichokes, plain lettuce and purple *feuille de chêne* lettuce, three sorts of apple and two of pear, bananas, apricots, peaches, strawberries, redcurrants, raspberries, cherries, nectarines and plums.

This abundance of choice is taken for granted, of course. And just as the French feel they have the right to sniff, prod, poke and even taste what is before them, they expect the highest standards of quality produce. They require their local greengrocer's wares to be irreproachably good, and are willing to pay for it. For more modest budgets, even the largest hypermarkets will stock great-tasting locally produced fruit and vegetables.

Studies into the 'French Paradox' (see page 31) have found that fruit and vegetables were the only types of food for which Gallic portion size was considerably bigger than in other countries. Getting 'five a day' can sometimes happen in one sitting! Fruit and veg regularly appear at least three times in any French meal: as crudités before the main course, then cooked plainly (braised or steamed) as a dish served after the meat or fish. A palate-refreshing green salad with chopped fresh herbs is often served before the cheese, and post-cheese fruit is usually eaten raw or simply poached in a home-made compote. At simple weekday winter meals, many French children are served home-made vegetable soup cooked from a base of root vegetables and varied with whatever is in season. In spring and summer, melon or sliced tomatoes are served practically every other day.

When I am too lazy to take out my knife and chopping board, the wonderful Picard frozen-food chain comes to my rescue with over 150 sorts of ready-prepared vegetable dishes to choose from. As an example, artichokes come in deleaved and debearded hearts, or baby-size and cut into quarters, or puréed, or cooked in three different all-veg dishes.

The perceived drudgery attached to preparing vegetables from scratch somehow seems an alien concept to most French women, but Picard has been the shameful saviour of many a French working mum's evening meal – it is now becoming more acceptable to use frozen produce.

Fewer French women than in the past prepare and sterilise pots of home-grown green beans or peas, but many still make their own jam. I was surprised that in Scotland I had to find a specialist cook store to buy jam jars, despite the abundance of raspberries and strawberries. In France, every supermarket stocks basic jam-making and preserving equipment.

Tarte aux poireaux et reblochon

Baby leek and reblochon pie

A quick way of using those dinky mini vegetables invading UK supermarkets but which are still rare in France because the French don't need gimmicks to eat their greens. This also works well with baby red onions or spring onions.

FOR 4

About 20 baby leeks

4 squares of ready-rolled puff pastry, about 15 x 15 cm each

1 'ripe' reblochon cheese (or you could use camembert, or saint nectaire or anything creamy and pungent)

4 tablespoons crème fraîche

Salt and freshly ground black pepper

Preheat the oven to 180°C/350°F/gas mark 4.

Blanch the leeks in boiling water for about 5 minutes. Drain and cool.

With the tip of a sharp knife, but without cutting through the pastry completely, score a square about 2 cm in from the edge of the pastry for each piece. This will make the sides puff up more when cooking.

Slice the cheese finely and set the slices in the centre of each pastry square. Spread the crème fraîche over the cheese and then set the leeks on the cream, lining them up evenly – cut off their tops if they are untidily reaching over the edge of the pastry. Season with salt and pepper and bake for 10–15 minutes, until the pastry is golden and the cheese bubbling into the cream.

Serve with a crisp salad.

Velouté de lentilles vertes du Puy aux noisettes

Cream of Puy lentil soup with hazelnuts

Green Puy lentils have a lot going for them. They are practical, cooking more quickly than other varieties and with no need for soaking beforehand. Their taste is distinctive, sweet and nutty. They are also very good for you, rich in fibre, calcium, vitamins and iron. Total respect is demanded, therefore, when you cook such a superfood. A creamy soup is the simplest way, though Puy lentils also make a fantastic accompaniment to foie gras, game, ham and cooked smoked sausages.

FOR 4

10g butter

1 tablespoon olive oil

30g lardons, smoked if possible

1 carrot, chopped

1 medium onion, finely chopped

1 shallot, finely chopped

Sprig of thyme

1 bay leaf

220g Puy lentils

100g *crème fraîche épaisse* (see pages 40–41)

3–4 tablespoons chopped roasted hazelnuts

1 tablespoon chopped flat-leaf parsley

Salt and freshly ground black pepper

Heat the butter and oil in a large heavy-based pan and brown the lardons and the vegetables for a few minutes until golden, tossing in the thyme and bay leaf early on.

Add the lentils, cover with water, bring to the boil, cover, then simmer on a low heat for around 40 minutes. Add more water if it dries too quickly.

Remove the thyme and bay leaf and liquidise the soup in a food-processor. Stir in the cream, check the seasoning, garnish with the hazelnuts and parsley, and serve.

Salade très verte à la sucrine comme à l'Hôtel Costes

Hotel Costes' very green salad

The Costes family's reign on the Paris café scene began in the mid 1980s. Since then the glamorous, celebrity-fuelled lure of their restaurants and hotels has not waned. They invented 'le before', somewhere cool to eat lightly before continuing the evening elsewhere. Hotel Costes became an institution, unbearably noisy and *m'as-tu-vu* (showy, flashy) after midnight and during the Fashion Weeks that kept it famous, yet slick and discreet as an all-day hideaway for those needing quiet and calm with kudos in the heart of Paris.

Of the Costes establishments, French designer Andrée Putnam said: 'They have certainly helped to keep the Parisian population slim', so spartan did the food seem. But two decades on and the food has dated even less than a Birkin bag. For its timelessness was the whole point, and the one many Parisians didn't and still don't get. The menu is at once familiar, classic, international, luxurious, vegetarian, indulgent, fast, slow, super-spicy or boringly bland. There is a super-fresh sole meunière, with or without the *beurre noisette*; a perfect steak haché with chips and potato purée from every Frenchman's childhood; home-made pancakes with maple syrup and butter; and a bowl of aromatic *Mara des Bois* strawberries. The ham is AOC, the caviar beluga. Every dish is uneventful but properly done; it won't blow your mind, but it is exactly how your mind imagined it would be.

The Hotel Costes *salade toute verte* (fresh green salad) is beautifully presented, copious, easy to eat with a fork, and served with optional bread; the additional conceptual jokey element built around the contrast with an ordinary *salade verte* makes it into a dish when you don't want to 'have lunch', you just want sustenance.

For 4

2 sucrine lettuces (or the tightly packed hearts of any fresh lettuce)

400–500g of a variety of green vegetables, such as peas, green beans, courgettes, broad beans, runner beans, asparagus, broccoli and mangetout

4–6 tablespoons best-quality extra virgin olive oil

2 tablespoons lemon juice

Salt and freshly ground black pepper

Steam each type of vegetable separately, retaining the maximum crunch for each. Leave to cool slightly.

Cut the lettuce and arrange the vegetables around it into quarters.

Drizzle with olive oil and lemon juice, season with salt and pepper, and serve.

Choux de Bruxelles aux marrons, saumon fumé

Brussels sprouts with chestnuts and smoked salmon

A great accompaniment to game, or a quick and easy main course in itself.

FOR 4–6

500g brussels sprouts

75g butter

100g chestnuts, peeled and cooked

150g smoked salmon, in chunks or flakes

Fleur de sel and black pepper

Steam the brussels sprouts for 20 minutes or so, until they are well cooked but retain a bit of bite.

Toss the sprouts with the butter, crumble in the chestnuts and, finally, stir in the smoked salmon. Season and serve immediately.

Pommes sarladaises

Potatoes sautéed in garlic and goose fat

Sarlat-la-Canéda, a beautiful medieval town in the Périgord region of Dordogne, gave its name to this simple dish of sliced potatoes cooked with garlic in goose or duck fat. A luxurious version uses black truffles; here I have given a cep option. It may be hard to contemplate, but this is traditionally served alongside confit of duck. It's a good way of using the fat that the confits are encased in when bought preserved in a tin.

FOR 4–5

1kg waxy potatoes, such as Charlotte, Jersey Royal, Pink Fir Apple

3–4 tablespoons goose or duck fat

250g fresh cep mushrooms, coarsely chopped (optional)

2 whole garlic cloves

Chopped fresh curly parsley, to garnish

Salt and pepper

Wash, peel and cut the potatoes into thin slices. Cook them in gently boiling, salted water for 10 minutes.

In a heavy-based saucepan, heat the goose fat and fry the mushrooms. Add the garlic and the potatoes. When they are nice and golden, reduce the heat and let the mushrooms and potatoes cook in the fat and garlic for a further 10 minutes or so to infuse with their flavours.

They should be served somewhere between crispy and fondant, garnished with chopped parsley with salt and pepper to taste.

Asperges rôties, sauce aux oranges sanguines

Roasted green asparagus with blood orange sauce

Green asparagus is very good roasted. The tips caramelise beautifully and the stalks stay pleasingly moist. Outside the blood orange season, ordinary oranges will be fine.

FOR 4

400–500g green asparagus

2–3 tablespoons olive oil

1/2 shallot, very finely chopped

Juice of 2 blood oranges

100g lightly salted butter, very cold, cut into cubes, plus extra for frying

Fleur de sel (sea salt)

Preheat the oven to 180°C/350°F/gas mark 4.

Spread the asparagus in a roasting tin and drizzle with the olive oil. Roast for about 20 minutes or until the tips are crispy and the stalks a little wizened. Remove from the oven, season with a little *fleur de sel*, arrange on the plate or plates and prepare the sauce as they cool.

In a small pan, melt a small knob of butter and sweat the shallot very gently until it is soft. Add the orange juice, bring to the boil, then simmer gently until it has reduced by about half and becomes syrupy.

Remove the pan from the heat and whisk the cubes of butter into the reduced juice, making the sauce nice and airy. You can do this over a bain-marie (double boiler) if you wish, or more carefully over a direct heat.

Pour the frothy sauce over the asparagus and serve.

Salade d'oranges à la fleur d'oranger

Orange flower water scented orange salad

A simple and refreshing way to end a meal, especially if couscous or tagine came before. Serve the oranges with Moroccan pastries if you can find them.

FOR 4

5 juicy oranges
1 tablespoon orange flower water
Fresh mint, to decorate

Scrub the oranges well. Remove the zest of one of the oranges and squeeze its juice.

Squeeze a further 2 oranges and slice the remaining 2 into very fine slices. Mix the slices with the juice.

Flavour with the orange flower water and chill thoroughly for 2–3 hours.

Decorate with mint sprigs if you wish.

Piperade

Braised peppers with ham and eggs

This famous pepper, garlic and tomato stew, served with eggs and ham, is another French dish infused with disagreement. For a start, never call it French. It is one of the most emblematic Basque dishes, slow-cooked and rustic: sweet, hearty and piquant. The divergence of opinion comes from what type of peppers should be used and the role the eggs should play. The purists banish red or multi-colour and insist on only green, and at that the little green 'piments' popular in the Basque country. Versions exist with the vegetables folded through the eggs cooked in a loose omelette, others with scrambled eggs served beside the stewed peppers. All, however, seem to include great slabs of fried and salty Basque ham.

You could do a very light noughties rendition (the sort of thing Gordon Ramsay would cook in his 'Kitchen Challenge' to gleefully humiliate a home cook from Bayonne), Basquing up the peppers with *piquillos* and *piment d'Espélette*, setting a poached egg atop and wafer-thin Serrano ham cooked to crisp on the side.

All this pre-debating, conscious or not, is of course in itself extremely French and to French people is as vital an ingredient as salt and pepper. Our confident French home cook will eventually plump for a recipe that suits herself and the produce she knows she has to hand. This one comes from *cuisinière extraordinaire*, Louisette, in Vendée of all places, and was the way I first tasted piperade.

FOR 4

2 red peppers (or better, 3 long, sweet red peppers)

2 green peppers

4 ripe tomatoes (or a 300 g tin of good-quality passata)

Olive oil

3 garlic cloves, finely chopped

Good pinch of piment d'Espélette (or a small red chilli if you don't have the real thing)

6 medium eggs, beaten

4 slices of Jambon de Bayonne, or Spanish ham

Salt and freshly ground black pepper

Deseed the peppers and cut them into long strips.

Skin, quarter and deseed the tomatoes.

Heat the oil in a large heavy-based frying pan and cook the peppers and the garlic for 3–4 minutes, on a low heat, to soften them. Add the tomatoes, the piment and a little water, and let the whole thing simmer gently and reduce for about 20 minutes.

Season with salt and pepper (not too much salt as the ham will be salty).

In a separate saucepan, on a medium heat, cook the eggs, stirring from time to time with a wooden spoon until they are lightly scrambled.

Grill or fry the ham and serve with the eggs and vegetables on a large platter for everyone to help themselves.

Soupe au pistou

Pistou soup

A healthy, hearty soup, similar to the great Italian minestrone and a sure-fire way of letting a little southern French sunshine into your kitchen. Pistou, similar to Italian pesto, is a basil and garlic purée. I like the calming, cumulative aspect of this recipe. The chopping time of each ingredient lets those already in the pot cook perfectly so you never feel you are wasting your energy on a boring chore.

FOR 6

500 g dried white and red beans (unless you can find fresh coco and red beans)

300 g fresh green beans

300 g carrots

3 potatoes

3–4 courgettes

1 small leek, tough green bits removed

1 large tomato

100 g very small pasta (coquillettes, vermicelli or spaghetti broken into 1 cm pieces)

2 level tablespoons of freshly grated parmesan cheese, to garnish

FOR THE PISTOU

3 garlic cloves

1 large bunch basil

150 ml olive oil

2 level tablespoons of freshly grated parmesan cheese

Soak the red and white beans overnight in water. (No shortcuts permitted here, they are the soup's most important ingredient, after the basil in the pistou.)

Bring about 2 litres of water to the boil in a large saucepan, cover and cook the beans for about 1 hour.

Wash, top and tail the green beans, then dice them. Add them to the beans in the saucepan. Clean and peel the carrots, dice them finely and add them to the pot. Do the same with the potatoes.

Wash and dice the courgettes, without peeling them, and wash and dice the leek. Skin the tomato (dip it into boiling water for a minute then peel off the skin), cut into quarters and remove its pips, then cut the remaining flesh into small cubes. Add all three vegetables to the soup.

Half cover the saucepan with its lid and let the whole lot cook very gently for about 1 hour.

While it is simmering, prepare the pistou. (It too will benefit from a little time to let the basil deliciously infuse into the crushed garlic and olive oil.)

With a pestle and mortar, or in a small food-processor, crush the garlic cloves with the basil and oil, then add the parmesan and mix.

After the soup has been bubbling away for an hour, add the pasta and cook it for about 10 minutes, or according to the instructions on the packet.

Swirl the pistou into the soup, stir well and sprinkle with a little parmesan.

Inhale.

Carpaccio de melon au limoncello et huile d'olive

Melon carpaccio with limoncello and olive oil

Doesn't sound hugely French, I hear you mutter. But the combination is heavenly. It also demonstrates how glam a dish can suddenly sound when it is elevated from 'thinly sliced' to 'carpaccio'.

FOR 4

The ripest, most pungent large
   Charentais melon you can find,
   or 2 baby ones
A few drops of Limoncello liqueur
A few drops of mild extra virgin
   olive oil

Chill the melon well and slice it as thinly as you can, just before serving.

Drizzle with Limoncello and olive oil and serve.

Poires pochées au vin marocain cardamone, vanille, cannelle

Pears poached in moroccan wine with oranges, cardamom, vanilla and cinnamon

Pears poached in wine are a popular dessert in France, and it must be one of the most consistently bland and disappointing I come across. It really takes an intensely aromatic poaching syrup to give them some personality. This recipe does just that. The syrup has a lot of sugar, granted, but this is offset by the orange juice and zest, and creates a wonderful dark and shiny glaze. If you can't find Moroccan wine, use anything else full-bodied and full of sun.

FOR 4

1 bottle Moroccan red wine
300g caster sugar
2 cinnamon sticks
1 vanilla pod
2 cardamom pods
Juice of 2 oranges, plus the zest from
   one of them in large strips
1 orange, skin on, cut into 4 or 5 slices
4 ripe pears

In a casserole dish with a lid, bring the wine to the boil with the sugar, the spices, the orange juice, orange slices and zest.

Peel the pears, leaving some of the stalk. Stand them in the flavoured wine, cover, reduce the heat and poach them in the wine for about 40 minutes, basting as often as possible, or until the pears are cooked but still holding their shape.

During cooking, the poaching liquid will become more and more syrupy. If the pears are cooked before the syrup has reduced enough for your taste, remove them and give it a bubble until you are happy. Leave to cool.

Serve the pears with the orange slices and sauce poured around them.

Offal and Game

Opposite, clockwise from top left: Calf's head and cock's crest. Hare. Boudin noir. Lambs' kidneys. Onglet. Roast boar.

This is where our French cooks' lack of squeamishness becomes most apparent. Cuts classed as offal are sold alongside muscle and bone in the usual shops: at the poultry shop are chicken liver, foie gras and *gésier* (gizzard); at the *charcuterie* and at the butchers' are ears, tripe, tongue, trotters, liver, cheeks, kidneys and various innards made into sausages and pâté. Veal sweetbreads are considered to be the most refined and delicate of treats. They were much lamented during the BSE-scare ban on offal, and when it was lifted there was nationwide rejoicing.

Specialised *tripiers*, the hardcore offal sellers, still exist. Their clientele is made up of discerning nose-to-tail-eating fans or, as with horse meat, much older customers than in everyday meat shops, reflecting how taste and habits have evolved with the growing abundance of quality cuts since the Second World War.

The dapper elderly couple who run the tripe stall in the Saint-Germain market have become my pals. They are bursting with pride to talk about their trade, their wares and how to cook them, and have given me countless tips and recipes over the years. From them I buy lean, melting pig and beef cheeks for slow-cooking in cider and wine, ox heart for the barbecue and tiny lamb's livers for a quick turn in the pan with onions and bay. They sell veal or beef *onglet*, a stringy yet succulent part that connects the stomachs of ruminants (such as cattle and sheep) and is cooked as you would any steak. My cultural programming still makes me draw the line at more extreme bits, however. Maybe one day I will try cooking calf's or lamb's brain or the euphemistically named 'white kidneys' from male calves.

Game is also considered a delicacy, if rather old-fashioned. Much of France's game is now farmed, but hunting certainly does not look set to disappear. The hunting lobby has a significant political presence, in the French regions, forming a party called Chasse, Pêche, Nature, Traditions. Though its voice is often a radical one, it considers itself to be rural France's mouthpiece and the sworn enemy of France's Greens. Anti-hunting public opinion is increasing, but rather than being based on thoughts of animal welfare it seems more focused on reclaiming France's public forests over which hunters roam, causing many accidents and discouraging walkers.

When we lived in the country, neighbours who hunted had a habit of presenting me with dead pheasant, ducks and bits of boar or deer that invariably needed a combination of beheading, dehoofing, skinning, gutting or hanging. I was inwardly horrified yet also flattered as these were rare and precious gifts that expressed trust in my cooking skills and hope of an invitation to share in the cooked version. It was as if I had passed some sort of 'Asterix and Obelix meet the Anglo-Saxons' initiation rite into a country tribe. A great believer in delegating, I developed a secret network of ladies in my village and nearby who would prepare them properly or even swap for 'one they had prepared earlier' (smaller, of course, they were canny, but then, who would remember?).

Nowadays, just as most French cooks do, I buy my game pre-prepared, just as I would any other meat at Monsieur Janinet's (see page 21).

Salade d'oreilles et groin de cochon

Pig's ear and snout salad

Tripe is becoming very trendy in France in much the same way as Jerusalem artichokes, salsify, swede and parsnips and other 'forgotten' vegetables are now featured on the swankiest of menus. These post-world-war ingredients, for many years synonymous with hardship and restrictions, are being rediscovered, and today they are cooked using very different methods to those in the late 1940s and 50s.

I don't know how easy it is to find poached pig's ear and snout where you live, but in France it will require a team effort between you and your *charcutier* to make a go of this seemingly challenging dish. First up, don't be fooled into thinking you'll find these particular bits *chez le tripier* (at the tripe butcher), for the hierarchy between pig, calf, sheep and cow is a mysterious business. My *tripier* can sell me raw calf's ears but not pig's. He will sell me pig's cheeks but my *charcutier* will not, even though he cooks them in his terrine. And then everyone seems to sell boudin noir, even my cheesemonger.

Pig's ears go down very, very well amongst grown-ups and kids alike. The taste is like full-flavoured bacon, and the texture is very pleasant, not gristly, not fatty but firm, flavoursome yet giving. It's a fantastic and conversation-provoking alternative to the suddenly ubiquitous pork scratching appetisers offered everywhere in the UK.

Once cooked, both ear and snout are still rather more hairy than I can put up with, however, and they do require a little *toilettage* (grooming) before serving. It's lovely at last to make a recipe out of a pig's ear instead of the other way around.

FOR 6–8

1 pig's ear and 1 pig's snout, cooked, chopped into fine strips
2–3 shallots, finely chopped
2 garlic cloves, finely chopped
Cider vinegar
Mixed leaves, for the salad
A handful of drained capers
Extra virgin olive oil
Freshly ground black pepper

Get the pan really hot and toss in the ear and snout, shallots and garlic. Cook for about 7–8 minutes, stirring frequently so that everything gets golden and crispy.

For serving as a main course, deglaze the pan with a dash of cider vinegar and stir well, scraping up the tasty bits stuck to the pan.

Mix the ear and snout mixture with the salad leaves. Sprinkle the salad with the capers, add a little cider vinegar and olive oil and season with pepper – no need for salt.

To serve as an appetiser, deglaze the pan or not, as you wish. If you do you will lose a little crispness but gain a little interesting flavour and acidity which do help to cut through the fattiness. When the strips of ear and snout are golden, simply drain on some kitchen paper and serve with cocktail sticks or small forks.

Joues de porc braisées au cidre

Pig cheeks braised in cider

FOR 6–8

**2 tablespoons olive oil, plus extra
  for frying**
50g butter
1kg pig's cheeks
4–5 shallots
750ml dry cider
200g button mushrooms
Salt and freshly ground black pepper

Preheat the oven to 160°C/325°F/gas mark 3.

Heat the oil and butter in a heavy-based casserole with a lid. Brown the meat with the shallots for a few minutes, then pour over the cider and scrape the bottom of the pan to deglaze, bring to the boil and cover. Transfer to the oven and cook for 1 hour 30 minutes.

Some 20 minutes before serving, fry up the mushrooms in a little olive oil and add them to the casserole.

Serve with fresh ribbon pasta.

Boudin noir aux deux pommes

Black pudding with apples and potatoes

French black pudding is made from ham, pork offal, blood, fat and flavoured spices, usually cloves and pepper. Most recipes will tell you to cook the boudin separately from the apples, and often you will see it neatly served with the apple and potato purées on the side. But my children love this messy, unattractive way of presenting and eating the whole lot thrown in the pan together. Serve it with French mustard.

FOR 4

Olive oil, for frying

500–700 g black pudding, cut if necessary to fit your pan

4 waxy potatoes, cooked, peeled and sliced

4 Granny Smith or other tart apples, peeled and sliced

Heat a little oil in a frying pan and cook the black pudding for about 5 minutes, turning it over frequently until the outside is crispy all over. Add the potatoes and apples and continue to cook until golden for a further 7–8 minutes, stirring occasionally. Serve hot.

Pâté de foies de volaille aux baies de genièvre et cognac

Chicken liver pâté with juniper, bay and cognac

The traditional French way of making terrine is, of course, in a terrine. But I've spared you that as well as the additional pork, veal or chicken meat usually added to pad out the pâté.

FOR 4–5

150g butter

250g chicken livers

1–2 shallots, finely chopped

2 juniper berries

1 bay leaf

2 tablespoons cognac

Salt and freshly ground black pepper

Melt 30g or so of the butter in a frying pan and fry the livers with the shallots, juniper and bay for about 5 minutes, stirring often until the livers are golden on the outside but still pink inside.

Melt the rest of the butter and put in a blender with all the ingredients. Blend to a smooth paste, then transfer to small ramekins or one larger terrine. Serve with warm *pain de campagne* and some chutney.

Fromage de tête, sauce verte

Fromage de tête with green sauce

Fromage de tête – a literal translation would be 'head cheese' – is a jellied terrine made of pig's head meat, confirming the old French saying, 'Dans le cochon, tout est bon' – every part of a pig is good (for eating).

This is a quick serving idea that works well with many of the delicious pâtés and terrines tempting you in the *charcuterie*.

FOR 4 as a starter

1 thick slice *fromage de tête* or *jambon persillé* (jellied terrine of parsleyed ham)

Parsley, to garnish

FOR THE SALAD

100 g green beans, cooked and cooled

3–4 cornichons

2 Granny Smith apples

2 shallots

A handful of drained capers

Finely chop the beans, cornichons, apples and shallots and mix them together in a bowl. Stir in the capers.

Ganish the *fromage de tête* with parsley and serve with the salad.

Râble de lièvre rôti

Roast saddle of hare

I once made *Lièvre à la Royale*, jugged hare, from scratch. Two days of marinating and cooking the gamiest hare in the world. Never again. My kitchen, fridge, hands, hair all ended up steeped in the smell. I had to throw out the bowl I had used. And when it came to serving the dish, I couldn't bear to eat it. This is altogether a much cleaner, quicker, easier affair.

FOR 3

250 ml cognac
2 tablespoons olive oil
Sprig each of thyme and rosemary
1 garlic clove
2–3 juniper berries
2 bay leaves
1 saddle of hare (about 600 g)

The day before, pour all the marinade ingredients into a shallow dish, set the hare in it and baste it, then cover tightly with clingfilm. Leave it in the fridge overnight.

To cook the hare, preheat the oven to 200°C/400°F/gas mark 6.

Drain the hare from its marinade and place it in a roasting tin. Set the tin on the hob and brown the meat all over, then cover with foil and roast for 10–15 minutes. Let the hare sit for a good 10 minutes before slicing.

Hare is a powerfully flavoured meat, so serve it simply with some fruit chutney or cranberry sauce and fresh, buttered ribbon pasta.

Cocotte de sanglier au poivre, poires, chocolat et airelles

Roast boar with pepper, pears, chocolate and cranberries

Have no fear, this recipe is perfectly civilised and starts with the boar ready-prepared, neatly rolled into a roast-beef-shaped *rôti*. This is the way 90 per cent of Frenchwomen will purchase it from their butcher or even from the wonderful Picard frozen food store, rarely giving a moment's thought to how it got there.

FOR 6

1.5–2 kg fillet roast of boar, rolled and tied

200 g sugar, plus 2 tablespoons for cooking the cranberries

6 pears, fat and round rather than long and tall, not too ripe

6–8 tablespoons fresh cranberries

500 ml veal or beef stock, fresh if possible

2 small cinnamon sticks

3 tablespoons olive oil

30 g butter

50 g good-quality dark chocolate, minimum 70% cocoa solids, broken into small chunks

FOR THE MARINADE

750 ml full-bodied red wine

3 shallots, finely chopped

1 garlic clove, crushed

1 tablespoon freshly ground black pepper

1 bouquet garni

The day before cooking, prepare the marinade by mixing all the marinade ingredients together. Pour this into a large shallow dish, add the meat and roll to coat well. Cover with clingfilm and marinate in the fridge for 24 hours, turning the meat and basting it with the liquid as often as you can remember.

The next day, about 2 hours before your guests arrive, pour 500 ml water into a large pan, stir in the 200 g of sugar and bring to the boil. Peel the pears and poach them in the syrup for about 3–4 minutes, then let them drip dry and cool. Cut off the tops to form little hats and scoop out some flesh from each pear to form a nest for the cranberries.

In a small pan over a medium heat, cook the cranberries for 8–10 minutes until soft, in just a little water, adding the 2 tablespoons of sugar at the end to take the edge off their bitterness but without overly sweetening them.

Drain the marinade for the meat into a saucepan, add the veal or beef stock and the cinnamon, bring to the boil then simmer for about 40 minutes until reduced by half or more. You want it to have a satisfyingly saucelike consistency; only the meat cooking juices and the chocolate will be added later. Remove from the heat, discard the bouquet garni and cinnamon and set aside.

Meanwhile, preheat the oven to 150°C/300°F/gas mark 2. Fill the pear cavities with cranberries, cover each with its 'hat', place them in a roasting tin and generously drizzle a little of the reduced marinade and stock mixture over them. Roast for 20–25 minutes. Transfer the pears to a serving dish in which you can reheat them in the microwave or the oven just before serving.

About 1 hour before serving, preheat the oven to 180°C/350°F/gas mark 4. Heat the oil in a heavy-based pan and brown the meat all over. Transfer it to a snug roasting tin, top with the butter and roast for 40 minutes or so. Remove the roast from the oven and let it rest for a good 10–15 minutes before carving.

While the meat is resting, reheat the pears and prepare the sauce: drain the meat cooking juices into the reduced marinade and stock mixture, bring to the boil and add the chocolate, whisking it into the sauce as it melts. Remove immediately from the heat, check the seasoning and serve with the roast boar and pears.

Lapin au roquefort

Rabbit in blue cheese sauce

FOR 4–6

1 rabbit, cut into pieces by your butcher

2 tablespoons plain flour

50 g butter

2 tablespoons olive oil

2 onions, finely chopped

550 ml dry white wine

250 ml single cream

150 g blue cheese, such as bleu d'Auvergne, bleu des causes or cashel blue, broken into small pieces

Dust the rabbit pieces in flour. In a heavy-based saucepan, heat the butter with the oil. Add the rabbit and the onions and cook for a few minutes, stirring occasionally, to brown the meat.

Pour in the wine, scrape the bottom of the pan to deglaze, then reduce the heat to very low, cover, and let the rabbit simmer for about 40 minutes.

Add the cream and let the sauce bubble until it is nice and thick. Add the blue cheese and stir until it has melted into the sauce.

Serve with fresh pasta or boiled potatoes.

Bourguignon de biche de Coco

Coco's venison stew

This is my eldest son Coco's favourite dish, in fact a Frenchified version of one he first tasted in Gloucestershire. He is now 13, and as the shooting season starts he checks out when venison becomes available at Monsieur Janinet's shop on his way home from school. On Fridays we can buy the shop's ready-marinated version, but mainly we prefer to choose the wine that goes into the stew and make it all ourselves. The next step will be to get Coco to do all the cooking from start to finish.

FOR 6

1.5 kg venison shoulder, cut into bite-sized chunks by your butcher

2–3 tablespoons olive oil

1–2 tablespoons plain flour

2 carrots, thinly sliced

1 celery stick, cut into 6 chunks

FOR THE MARINADE

750 ml full-bodied red wine

2 bay leaves

3–4 juniper berries

1 large onion, sliced

Sprig of fresh thyme

Salt and black pepper

In a large, deep dish, mix all the marinade ingredients together. Add the venison and stir well to coat all the meat in marinade. Cover with clingfilm and marinate in the fridge for 24 hours.

Preheat the oven to 160°C/325°F/gas mark 3.

With a slotted spoon, remove the pieces of meat from the marinade and pat them dry with kitchen paper. Keep the marinade to one side.

Heat the oil in a large heavy-based casserole with a lid, roll the meat lightly in the flour and brown all over in the hot oil. Add the carrots and celery and continue cooking for 1–2 minutes. Pour in the marinade, stir and dislodge all the sticky tasty bits stuck to the bottom of the casserole, then bring to the boil.

Cover the casserole, transfer to the oven and cook for about 2 hours until tender, longer if necessary. Add water to the casserole if it starts to dry out during cooking.

Serve with redcurrant jelly, fresh ribbon pasta, green beans and boiled potatoes.

Pigeon comme une pastilla

Pastilla Pigeon

If you are ever invited to a Moroccan banquet, remember that pastilla is the *pièce de résistance*, coming after many courses of salads and often a tagine. It is placed in the centre of the table, and everyone tears small pieces off with their fingers. Breaking through the thin crust into the sweet and succulent pigeon beneath feels so sensuous and decadent that finding a little more appetite is easy.

Making it, however, is a time-consuming labour of love. My version leaves out the egg (useful really for binding the other ingredients), stopping short of the long and fiddly final construction phase, in which the buttered pastry is carefully folded around the already-cooked, crushed or shredded main ingredients before heading back into the oven.

FOR 2 but forget the starter

2 tablespoons olive oil

2 small pigeons

3 medium onions, finely chopped

3 teaspoons ground cinnamon, plus
   extra for dusting

1/2 teaspoon saffron strands

1 heaped tablespoon sugar

20g unsalted butter, melted

4 sheets of filo pastry

30g blanched whole almonds

Icing sugar, for dusting

Salt and freshly ground black pepper

Preheat the oven to 150°C/300°F/gas mark 2.

Heat the oil in a heavy-lidded casserole dish large enough to hold the pigeons snugly. Brown the birds and the onions for a few minutes. Add the ground cinnamon, a little salt, saffron, sugar and enough water to cover the pigeons' thighs. Put the lid on and cook in the oven for about 1 hour until tender and falling off the bone.

Prepare the pastry. With a pastry brush, spread the melted butter over the sheets of filo pastry. Pile them onto greaseproof paper in a baking tray.

Take the casserole out of the oven. Turn the oven up to 200°C/400°F/gas mark 6 for the pastry. Whizz the almonds in a food-processor (they taste better this way than when bought ready-chopped) and stir them into the casserole. Season to taste. Keep the casserole warm.

When the oven is hot, cook the pastry for about 5 minutes or until crisped and golden.

Dust the pastry with icing sugar and cinnamon, and serve with the pigeons.

Pastilla is Morocco's most sumptuous national dish, the one you will be served proudly on a special occasion, or if you are lucky enough to be considered an honoured guest. It is a fabulously rich pie, filled with pigeon, almonds, egg, onion, cinnamon and saffron, encased in paper-thin, sugar-dredged pastry.

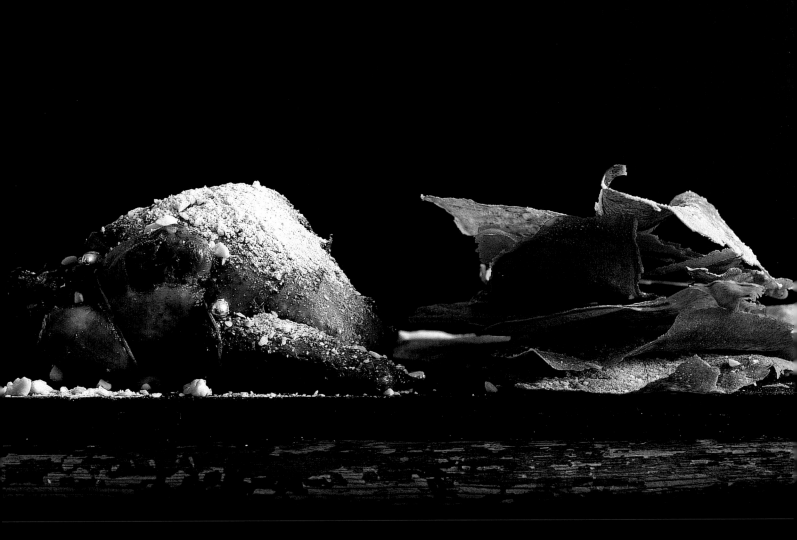

Épicerie fine

Opposite, clockwise from top left: Snails cooking at the market in St Rémy. Famous mustard from Meaux. Jams and cheese chez M. Dubois, delicacies to buy while on holiday to keep in your storecupboard. Picard frozen food store saves French cooks too! Pâté de canard from Périgord.

The lure of the designer label, the guarantee of new taste discoveries and the anticipated Laura Ingalls Wilder satisfaction of hoarding little tins, jars, packets and boxes of delicacies turn the *épicerie fine* into every food lover's treasure trove. You feel a great rush of excited expectation as you enter, greeted by a dozen mingled unfamiliar smells. The *épicerie fine* is one French food shop where browsing and indecision are considered normal, where it seems to be OK not to know this or that spice or pulse or dish. It is where French cooks top up their knowledge and their pantries. All *épicerie* fine owners worth their *fleur de sel* are helpful, patient and passionate about their goods.

The owner of the appropriately named Le Rameau d'Olivier (the Olive Branch) across the street from my home, literally dives out onto the pavement and pulls me in when he sees me going past and something new requiring tasting has arrived. On market days his shop is always crammed full. It becomes a mini food appreciation society, with everyone exchanging tips on what's hot at today's market, recipes and stories of how well what they bought last week went down. Once he gave me fresh, barely pasteurised green olives, a new way of serving them, firm and still full of sun. Before that we formally acknowledged the arrival and potential of dried strawberries. At Christmas I had to sample his foie gras and an amazing ancient distilled vinegar, poured into spoons and administered by hand by him as if I were eight years old and taking Veno's cough mixture.

Here, there is less fresh produce on offer than in the delicatessens in the UK, as all the fish and meat sellers already stock a lot of ready-prepared dishes, many of which they make themselves. Apart from luxury chains such as Fauchon and Hédiard, the hybrid *traiteur/épicerie fine* shops are the showcases of caterers who do most of their business outside normal trading hours and whose *épicerie fine* ranges are more restricted than *chez* purists like Le Rameau d'Olivier.

Often the fresh things sold in *épiceries fines* will be apéritif or tapas-style specialities such as tapenade (olive paste), anchoïade (anchovy paste), olives, perhaps a cheese or two, some fresh pasta, pâtés and terrines, and always excellent-quality dried and cured meats and hams.

These shops are where French cooks find the best-quality snails, anchovies, chestnuts, oils, vinegars, pulses, liqueurs, dried and sugared fruit, confits and rillettes. They will stock what is needed to cook North African dishes: preserved lemons, harissa paste, ras el hanout, orange flower water, pomegranate molasses and pistachios. Catering to the ultra-refined vision many French people have of teatime, they will sell the finest teas, meringues and macaroons, biscotti, *les cakes anglais* and bite-sized buttery madeleines and sablés.

The international section houses exotic oddities such as Colman's mustard powder, Lea & Perrins Worcestershire Sauce, lemon curd, crunchy peanut butter and Hershey's chocolate sauce. At the Rameau d'Olivier they are bought to comfort the town's English homesick au pairs. None of the French customers has the slightest idea what to do with them.

gastronomiquement incorrect
snails and frogs' legs

I have come across many French people who find snails and frogs' legs distasteful but many, many more who cannot see what the fuss is about. As with other 'taboo' dishes such as tripe, any repulsion is subliminally linked to the fact that these are scavenged, leftover foods which were once strongly associated with poverty and starvation, as opposed to gastronomy and culinary delight.

Today, scavengers have become gatherers, as hunger appears far down the list of why one should eat such animals as frogs and snails, which are now very rarely hunted in the wild and prepared from scratch at home. They are more likely to come from farms, many of which are outside France.

In Burgundy, my friends the Lena family still catch frogs the traditional way. There are several ponds around their beautiful old house in Chérizy, all overflowing with plump green and black frogs. A small piece of red cloth is attached to a fishing rod with a hook and dangled above the frog's barely visible nose poking out from the waterweed. It's a long process, for the noise made by one frog being hooked understandably scares the others off for quite a while. They are killed and skinned on the spot, and kept in some water and vinegar before being prepared for cooking.

The people of the world eat 200 million frogs' legs a year, most of which come from Indonesia, and France devours about half of those. That takes national consumption to about one leg a year per person, so consider the myth well and truly dead even if the nickname will stick for as long as the French call the British *rosbif*. In France, frogs are protected and the hunting season is extremely short. You can find frogs' legs fresh at fishmongers, lined up on skewers; these need to be soaked overnight in milk before being cooked. Mostly, however, they are bought frozen and simply sautéed in garlic, parsley and butter.

Snails, when properly produced, are tasty and meaty. In supermarkets, they come ready to cook on foil plates with little indentations. You will still need the special tongs for grasping them without burning your fingers, and the long, curved, two-pronged fork to poke out those hiding in the depths of their shells.

France is the world's biggest consumer of snails and they have remained a big part of daily French food, commonly offered as delicacies in traditional *bistros* and *brasseries*, and in fancier restaurants often part of sophisticated mixes including foie gras, puff pastry, sweetbreads and cream. They are mostly gathered in the wild, but snail farms are booming as demand for organic produce rises. There are now over 200 snail farms in France. The traditional region, however, is Burgundy, and the rich recipe *à la Bourguignonne*, a reference worldwide for preparing them in the shell with garlic butter, is most popular. It is rumoured, however, that this may change. In some subversive Parisian circles there is a story going round that an Englishman cooked them in porridge.

Cuisses de grenouilles, sauce au tamarin

Frogs' legs with tamarind and garlic cream

FOR 4

12 pairs of frogs' legs

3 tablespoons plain flour

Olive oil and butter, for frying

Fleur de sel (sea salt)

FOR THE TAMARIND CREAM

1 teaspoon tamarind paste

2 garlic cloves, crushed

150 ml single cream

Make this into a main course by adding some steamed crunchy broccoli and crushed hazelnuts.

In a mini food-processor, whizz together the tamarind paste and garlic. Transfer this paste to a small bowl and mix with the cream.

Turn the frogs' legs in the flour to coat them well. Heat some oil and butter together in a frying pan and fry the frogs' legs in batches as necessary until crisp and golden.

Drain any excess oil on kitchen paper, season with *fleur de sel* and serve with the tamarind cream as a dip.

Escargots à la Bordelaise

Snails cooked in wine and spices

The original recipe starts with: 'First, catch the snails. Then starve and purge them for three days.' If you are in the know, you can buy them alive in certain markets, starved and ready-purged. All you have to do is murder them in boiling vegetable stock then rinse off the foam, and they are ready for the recipe. Simple really.

Happily, mine come in jars from a small producer in Provence – dead, shelled, poached and preserved in a light herb broth. You will easily find them like this in large supermarkets and good *épiceries fines*.

This recipe is very, very tasty, if a little ingredient-heavy. But like frogs' legs, the meat must be strongly enhanced. It's a shame always to relegate our slimy friends to overwhelming garlic-butter baths, even if they come with the fun of the shells and all the paraphernalia.

I guess the only equivalent texture to a snail would be a whelk. There is something very satisfying about the round shape and firm give of a hot, spicy snail between your teeth.

FOR 4–6 as a starter or hefty apéritif

75g mild chorizo sausage

1/2 carrot

75g *poitrine fumée* (smoked bacon)

2 garlic cloves

1 onion

2 shallots

2 tablespoons olive oil

2 tablespoons cognac

About 60–70 ready-to-cook shelled snails (the tins and jars will usually say how many are inside)

1 tablespoon fennel seeds

2 sprigs of thyme

2 strips of orange zest

2 teaspoons dried ground pepper or cayenne

2 medium tomatoes, skinned and deseeded

750ml full-bodied red wine, such as Côtes du Rhône

Sprig of flat-leaf parsley, to garnish

Finely chop the chorizo, carrot, *poitrine*, garlic, onion and shallots. In a heavy-based saucepan, heat the oil and gently cook the chopped mixture for 3–4 minutes. When the onion is soft, add the cognac and scrape the bottom of the pan to deglaze. (It's not vital, as the alcohol will slowly work its way out of the dish, but you could flambé at this stage by igniting the cognac. Indeed, you may do so inadvertently if working with gas, so be careful.)

Drain the snails, add them to the saucepan and give it all a good stir. Then stir in the fennel seeds, thyme, orange zest, pepper or cayenne and the tomatoes. Pour in the wine and bring to the boil, then cover, reduce the heat and simmer for a good 1 hour 30 minutes, stirring frequently.

Serve garnished with parsley on some Poilâne malt bread.

Escargots au beurre d'ail

Snails with garlic and parsley butter

It's easy to make this dish in France: the snails are sold ready to cook, separately from the attractive, scrubbed stripy shells that are ready to rehouse their deceased ex-tenants, and the accompanying garlic butter comes neatly rolled in sausage shapes. You should be able to find snails and shells in specialist French food shops and some large supermarkets.

You will need the proper kit when serving this. Special plates with little indentations to hold the shells are available everywhere, as are the long pronged forks to poke them out with and tongs that save the tips of your fingers from being scalded.

FOR 6

**36 ready-to-cook shelled snails,
    plus 36 shells**

FOR THE GARLIC BUTTER

**400 g good-quality salted butter,
    slightly softened**
4 garlic cloves, peeled
Sprig of flat-leaf parsley
Juice and zest of 1 lemon

Preheat the oven to 190°C/375°F/gas mark 5.

Put the ingredients for the garlic butter into a food-processor and whizz for a few minutes until the butter takes on an attractive green hue and the lemon juice is as mixed in as it can be.

Drain the snails, put a small amount of the garlic butter into each shell, then insert a snail and seal each with a good knob of butter.

Fit the snail shells, butter side up, into their indentations and cook in the oven for 10 minutes or so until the butter is bubbling.

Leave to cool slightly before serving with lots of fluffy baguette to mop up the butter.

La truffe noire

Black truffles

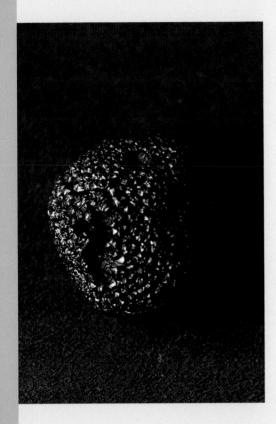

The perceived value of the truffle is so far removed from its real gastronomic value, so caught up in snobbery and fraud and glamour and hype, it was bound to give *Tuber melanosporum* a bad name. But the breathtakingly high prices charged for truffles (currently around 1,000 euros a kilo), can be better understood when one realises that truffle production is five hundred times lower than it was a hundred years ago and that current demand, even at that staggering price, is estimated as fifty times higher than supplies available.

The most noble species are *Tuber melanosporum*, the black Périgord truffle, and *Tuber uncinatum*, the Burgundy truffle. *Tuber brumale* and the Chinese truffle, *Tuber indicum*, are of much poorer gastronomic quality but can be more quickly cultivated. They look practically the same, however, and untrained noses can easily be tricked into buying them. The French agricultural authorities have devised a molecular test that can identify species in 48 hours.

Living one's life without ever smelling a fresh Périgord truffle would be to miss something incredible. It is supposed to be difficult to classify that primal, musky, damp-earth aroma. This is more to do with prudishness than lack of adequate prose. The first time they cast their spell on me was a January evening at the height of the season, at the Paris restaurant of Guy Savoy (Gordon Ramsay's French mentor). Someone at our table had ordered artichoke velouté, which was served adorned with wafer-thin petals of fresh *Tuber melanosporum* – their aroma arrived at our table a good five seconds before we even caught sight of the dish. Not usually prone to menu envy, I blessed my forthcoming main course choice of veal cutlet with brioche and *beurre aux truffes* (truffle butter). The melting butter provided the neutral, warm vehicle that released the truffle flavour into my mouth and nose, and I was hooked forever.

Those, to my mind, are the two best ways of serving black truffles. They need a neutral, creamy, earthy canvas and simple flavour combinations that accompany the truffle but cause as little distraction as possible. Eggs – whether scrambled, soft-boiled or in omelette form – love truffles shaved into them. Mushrooms, artichokes and root vegetables such as parsnip and celeriac work well, and luxurious meetings of lobster, scallop, langoustine and foie gras, raw or simply cooked with no complicated sauces in tow, also bring out the truffle's best qualities.

These qualities will keep only for up to a week after being harvested. They should be wrapped in layers of kitchen paper and left in a cool place; store them with eggs, which soak up the flavour through their porous shells, or with rice for a fantastic, simple risotto. If you absolutely have to preserve them, the best way to do so is to freeze them. Those sterilised in little jars have had the taste boiled out of them.

Parmentier de confit de canard aux cèpes et foie gras

Duck, cep and foie gras shepherd's pie

The *hachis parmentier* (a kind of shepherd's pie) is named after Antoine-Augustin Parmentier, a famous physician who introduced potatoes to France in 1771. Apart from the potatoes, all three ingredients in my version of the dish are classic *épicerie fine* products. This is a quick, easy and luxurious dish to master and serve.

FOR 4

500g floury potatoes, such as Maris Piper

3 tablespoons milk

75g butter

2 tinned *cuisses de canard confit* (confit duck's legs)

200g jar preserved cep mushrooms

1 shallot, finely chopped

50g tin or jar of *foie gras de canard* or *oie*

30g grated gruyère cheese

Boil the potatoes, then mash them into a soft purée with the milk and 50g of the butter.

While the potatoes are cooking, remove the duck confit from their tins and heat them in their delicious surrounding fat. Drain them, take the meat off the bones and pull it into small pieces.

Preheat the grill to hot.

Drain the ceps, heat the remaining butter in a frying pan and fry the mushrooms with the shallot. Mix them with the duck confit.

Crumble the foie gras through the cep and duck mixture and put it in a small gratin dish or four little ramekins. Top with the potato, sprinkle with cheese and brown under the grill.

Veau braisé aux citrons confits

Braised rose veal with preserved lemons

The more robust flavour of rose veal reared only on grass and its mother's milk goes well with potent preserved lemons and olives in this take on tagine. The dish would also work well with lamb or chicken.

FOR 6

2 tablespoons olive oil

1.5kg shoulder of veal, cut into chunks

2 medium onions, finely chopped

4 carrots, sliced

1 celery stick, cut into chunks

750ml veal or chicken stock

1 large or 2 small preserved lemons

Zest and juice of 1 lemon

150g pitted green olives

Salt and freshly ground black pepper

Preheat the oven to 180°C/350°F/gas mark 4.

Heat the oil in a heavy-based casserole dish and brown the meat on all sides with the onions, carrots and celery.

Add the stock, stir well to release any tasty bits that have stuck to the bottom of the pan, and bring to the boil. Add the preserved lemons and zest and juice, reduce the heat to low, cover and let the dish simmer very gently for about 1 hour 30 minutes.

About 10 minutes before serving, stir in the olives and let them heat through in the stew. Season to taste and serve.

Pimientos de piquillo à la brandade

Basque peppers stuffed with mashed cod, garlic and potatoes

Piquillos are small, sweet and smoky Basque peppers. They're easily found now that chefs such as Yves Camdeborde and Hélène Darroze have made south-western French specialities so popular. Brandade is halfway between a purée and an emulsion of salt cod, oil, garlic, and, sometimes, potatoes. It's available in tins or jars and most good fishmongers sell it, often home-made, in their *traiteur* section. If you can't find brandade, feta cheese with tuna is good. Ordinary roasted and peeled red peppers can be substituted for their smaller cousins.

FOR 4

**A small jar of piquillo peppers in oil
   (about 10 in a jar)**
400 g brandade

Drain the peppers and stuff them with a good tablespoon of brandade.

Serve chilled as a starter or hearty apéritif.

Gâteau aux pruneaux et à l'Armagnac

Prune and almond sponge with Armagnac crème fraîche

In *épiceries fines* the dried and sugared fruit are displayed irresistibly *en masse*. *Pruneaux* (prunes) are very popular, and are traditionally cooked with rabbit and pork and in Moroccan and Tunisian tagines. The ones to go for are the plump Agen prunes.

FOR 8

300 g pruneaux d'Agen, stoned
5–6 tablespoons Armagnac
150 ml crème fraîche
1 tablespoon caster sugar

FOR THE CAKE MIXTURE
175 g butter, softened
175 g caster sugar
3 medium eggs, beaten
150 g self-raising flour
50 g ground almonds

Put the prunes in a saucepan with a little water and half the Armagnac. Heat gently and simmer for 5 minutes or so, letting the prunes soften and plump up. Let them cool in the poaching liquid, then liquidise them in a food-processor.

Preheat the oven to 180°C/350°F/gas mark 4.

To make the cake, cream the butter and sugar together in a mixing bowl until the mixture whitens and becomes fluffy. Stir in the beaten eggs a little at a time. Fold the flour and ground almonds into the mix.

Lightly grease and flour eight dariole or muffin moulds. Alternatively, use a 'magic' silicone mould. Put a tablespoon of the cake mixture into each mould, and bake for about 15 minutes until risen and golden.

Mix the remaining Armagnac with the crème fraîche and the tablespoon of sugar.

Turn the sponge cakes out and serve warm with the prune purée and the flavoured cream.

Mont-Blanc

Crème de marrons with meringues and crème fraîche

The combination of meringue and chestnut purée is impossibly sweet. But their combined crumbliness and clogginess, offset by the smooth neutrality of cream, works. This recipe is a reminder that you can count on *épiceries fines* stocking good crème de marrons. They will keep well in your larder for when you need to whip up a last-minute dessert.

FOR 4

100 ml whipping cream
4 tablespoons sweetened chestnut purée
4 meringues or meringue shells

Whip the cream. Then either fold the chestnut purée into it, creating a swirled effect, and place a large dollop on the meringue, or keep them separate, and put a tablespoon of chestnut purée on the meringue and some whipped cream on top.

Fraises et oranges à la fleur d'oranger et à la menthe

Moroccan orange-flower scented strawberries and orange with mint

FOR 4–6

200 g unsalted butter
300 g plain flour
75 g ground almonds
75 g icing sugar, plus extra for dusting
2 tablespoons orange flower water

FOR THE FRUIT SALAD

200 g strawberries, thinly sliced
4 oranges, peeled
1 tablespoon orange flower water
Sprigs of mint, to decorate

Preheat the oven to 180°C/350°F/gas mark 4.

To make the biscuit dough, melt the butter in the microwave or in a small saucepan. Put the flour in a mixing bowl and add the ground almonds, icing sugar, orange flower water and the melted butter. Mix well with a spoon, then knead the dough with your hands for 1–2 minutes until it becomes smooth.

Line a baking tray with baking parchment, or set out a silicone mat. Divide the dough into about 20 pieces of equal size. Roll them into balls between your palms, then set them on the prepared tray or mat, and flatten them slightly. Bake for 20 minutes or so. Remove them from the oven and leave to cool, then dust with icing sugar.

As the biscuits are cooking, prepare the fruit salad. Put the sliced strawberries into a mixing bowl.

Divide the peeled oranges into segments. Working over the bowl of strawberries to collect any dripping juices, cut down the side of each segment with a sharp knife and remove its skin, then drop the flesh into the bowl. When you have extracted all the flesh, squeeze out into the bowl any remaining flesh in the skins.

Mix in the orange flower water and let the flavours mingle and develop as the biscuits cook and cool.

Serve the salad decorated with the mint sprigs, with the biscuits on the side.

Baked goods and sweet treats

Opposite, clockwise from top left: Mythical macaroons from Ladurée. Historically correct biscuits from Le Petit Duc. Chocolats Bonnat, some of the finest in France. Elegant baguettes from Poujauran. Nostradamus's nibbles. Joël Durand's chocolates, ready to be put in alphabetical order.

Every dedicated French cook has her 'little black book' of bought-in treats and accessories that make her meals special. Top-quality chocolate is still bought mostly at individual *chocolatiers*. It is a tradition to give beautiful boxes to friends and neighbours at Christmas. And at Easter, chocolate eggs, bunnies, chickens and, oddly, lobsters, are bought from local shops. Industrially made versions are thankfully confined to the bigger supermarkets.

The best local *pâtisserie* or *chocolatier* will provide a class-act dessert served as proudly as if it were home-made. For big occasions, such as weddings, Christmas, 14th July (Bastille Day) and the August bank holiday, cakes will be ordered well in advance, from the best shop in town or a big name such as Fauchon, Dalloyaux, Pierre Hermé or Ladurée.

Any decent *pâtissier* in even the smallest town can prepare a *pièce montée*, a centrepiece cake. The most traditional is a pyramid sculpture of little choux filled with *crème pâtissière* and held together with hardened spun caramel. It is set on a firm base of nougatine, with the appropriate greetings often written in sugar on another piece, crowning the whole spectacular work of art.

Another classic gateau, common at summer gatherings, is the *fraisier*. This is a sponge with butter cream, fresh strawberries and pastel green almond paste. It has a smooth, clear surface, allowing elaborate writing and patterns to be piped on in fondant.

But the most important address on the list will be the baker's shop, for even if the Atkins and South Beach diets have taken their toll in France too, bread is still fiercely defended as a birthright. It always amuses and amazes me to see queues full of sharp suits, stilettos and briefcases waiting patiently to tuck their evening baguette under their arm on their way home from work.

In France, bread is still eaten at every meal. The trend is currently towards healthier grains. Wholemeal, stoneground and organic loaves and baguettes are gaining 'territory'. As are *pain anglais*, muffins, pancakes and crumpets, although they are mainly to be found in supermarkets.

A few years ago the government brought in legislation that effectively saved part of France's culinary heritage. The name *boulangerie* can now be given only to shops where the bread is mixed, kneaded, risen and cooked on the premises. This distinguishes them from big chains such as La Brioche Dorée and Paul, most of whose produce is delivered frozen from a central factory and simply cooked in ovens in the shops (with the fabulous smells being fanned out onto the street!). It is a measure of how fiercely the French defend their Frenchness. Actively protecting small shopkeepers from powerful competition can be read as an example of how impervious France is to *la mondialisation* – globalisation. It is unthinkable that small local bakers should disappear from the French landscape.

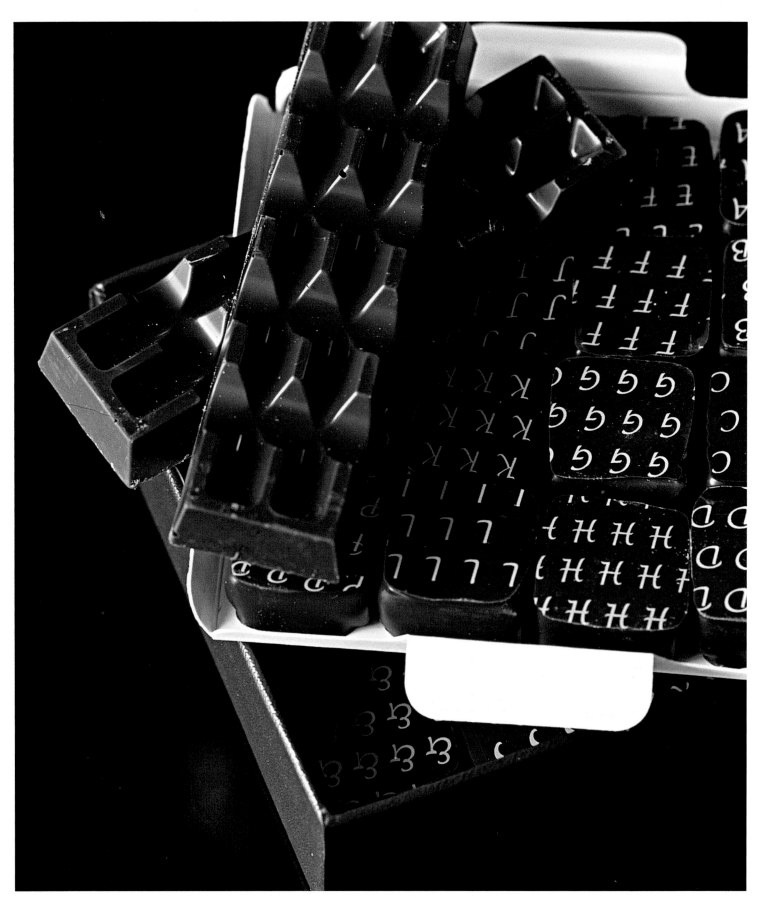

Chocolate
Joël Durand, Saint-Rémy-de-Provence

If you bring wine to a French dinner party don't expect to drink it there. It's a rather clumsy gift, a *cadeau empoisonné* (poisoned present). The chances are your hosts have already carefully thought through what they would like you to drink and your bottle won't suit the food being served. Champagne (chilled of course) is another matter, much easier to share pre-dinner or with pudding. If you lack the time or inspiration to find a thoughtfully personalised gift for Madame, bringing a box of chocolates is always a good idea. An added advantage, if you are greedy and curious, is that it is considered bad manners not to open and share them at the end of the meal.

You'll find yourself seated next to Madame or Monsieur as No.1 guest of honour if you bring them a box from La Maison du Chocolat, Jean Paul Hévin, Joël Durand or Pierre Marcolini. They are France's most famous chocolate *créateurs*. Their chocolates are intricate jewels to the *pâtissiers' haute couture* cake collections. New flavours and shapes are announced in the fashion and luxury press with as much fuss as the latest Rolex or Chloé handbag.

Joël Durand's tablettes from Saint-Rémy-de-Provence are the prettiest. Designed as rows of tiny, blunt crocodile teeth, to help yours bite into them and your palate taste them more efficiently, they are delicately flavoured with Provençal herbs and flowers – perfect with end-of-evening herbal teas, espressos and cognacs.

Durand is originally from Brittany but in the mid-1990s his love of Provence brought him to Saint-Rémy, where he set up shop and home. Like his chocolate, Durand is complex and irresistible. As sensitive and nervous as a Prix de l'Arc de Triomphe thoroughbred, with intense mahogany eyes, dark curls and long hands, he could be a male version of Juliette Binoche's character in the film *Chocolat*. Passionately defensive of his know-how, like many French food artisans he is also viciously quick in trashing the competition, melodramatically denouncing their methods and calling them *imposteurs*. His is an attitude I have seen over and over among French chefs and artisans, many of whose work borders on genius.

To speak the language of chocolate, Durand explains, one must start with an alphabet. How obvious. His collection of identically formed square ganache is identified with 26 letters and 6 punctuation marks, each ganache imagined and developed with infinite care and detail.

Naturally, A is a straight dark, 70 per cent ganache, encased, as is the rest of the collection, in a fine coating of 66 per cent cocoa chocolate. Its purpose is simply to test your mouth's tasting apparatus. From B onwards, the festival begins: combinations of Corsican honey, cloves and fresh lemon zest, jasmine tea, spearmint, praline made from Piedmont hazelnuts and even olives from the nearby Vallée des Baux. These softly and subtly caress the taste buds, but never overpower the chocolate ganache melting smoothly and unctuously on the tongue.

Sometimes, however, it's better to bite and chew than swirl. Take, for instance, T for Tiramisu: coffee, mascarpone and biscuit magically, deliciously all appear then fade one after the other as you taste. The layering and order of texture and taste is not an accident but exactly as Joël meant it to be.

Joël's most jealously guarded secret is how he extracts aromas from the freshest of herbs and spices. He doesn't use them fresh and direct, he doesn't dry them out and grind them down, nor does he use pure essential oils. His magical technique, whatever it may be, is used to perfection in the even more sophisticated punctuation-mark ganaches, which are available only for the time their star flavour is in season.

Biscuits and confectionery
Le Petit Duc, Saint-Rémy-de-Provence

The biscuits and confectionery at Le Petit Duc are typical of those the French like to serve with dessert, afternoon tea or post-prandial coffee. They know that interesting accessories will always glamorise home-made ice cream, compote, fruit salads and mousses. In their crammed 'laboratory', Anne Daguin and her husband Hermann Van Beeck create the most intellectually satisfying traybakes you will ever taste. Each sablé, macaroon, nougat, calisson and croquant is first cooked in its own history. Many of the recipes have their roots in the experimental works with sugar by the sixteenth-century physician and astrologer, Nostradamus. Others come from the secret recipe book of Pol Adam, the early twentieth-century French pastry chef to Belgian king Albert I, pages of which Anne Daguin cajoled from his granddaughter. Perhaps the most touching archive she uses was found for her by a Saint-Rémy bookseller. It is a set of recipes compiled as a wedding present for his grandmother by Marie Gachet, daughter of Van Gogh's friend and benefactor, Dr Gachet.

Anne Daguin says of her creations: 'In a recipe, a process or an ingredient, I love to find the people who contributed to them. Their contributions are of all kinds, perhaps some writing, a conversation, a product, a tool, a perfume, an image… Eating keeps us alive, sharing our food makes the food better, knowing what we are eating and why keeps the connection with past generations, in telling its story we pass all this on to our children.'

Le Petit Duc is on the busy outer edge of the dense labyrinth that is old Saint-Rémy-de-Provence. Its chic, spartan windows, dappled by plane trees, sit boldly three doors down from Joël Durand's chocolate store (see previous pages). It seems extraordinary that two of France's most gifted food craftsmen, neither of whom is native to Provence, should have ended up practically side by side. One might presume they have much in common, but their singular, driven personalities keep the closeness purely physical. It's a little like the relationship that exists between a chef and a pastry chef (Anne's father and her husband, for example), which she describes as 'respect mutuel, incompréhension totale': mutual respect and utter miscomprehension.

Anne and Hermann make an original team. Anne, a passionate food historian, researches and develops the old recipes. She is the youngest daughter of a famous French gastronomical dynasty. Her father owned a two-Michelin-starred hotel-restaurant in the south-western town of Auch for 40 years and is now an outspoken politician. Hermann, a pastry chef from Germany, fiercely reigns over his laboratory, where Anne's findings are painstakingly tested and translated into their exquisite edible form. Just as in ancient times, sugar is used as a preservative, not a taste, and the resulting biscuits are refined and subtle to the extreme. Without an overpowering sweetness dulling the taste buds, vanilla, almond, saffron, fennel, lavender, thyme and pepper lightly but distinctly flavour the perfectly balanced crumbly, crunchy and caramelised textures. The fifteen or so dainty creations come shaped as hearts, clover, flowers, stars and new moons to match romantic names like Folie de Paulette, Désiré, Coeur du Petit Albert, and Lune.

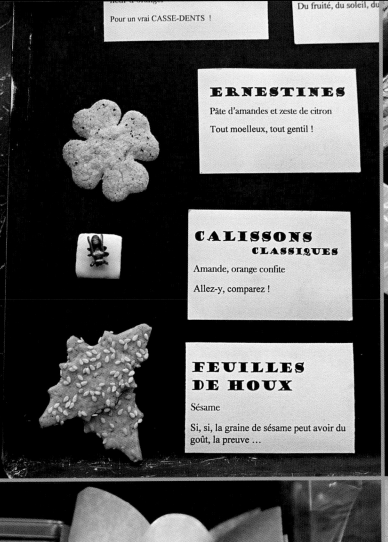

Pour un vrai CASSE-DENTS !

Du fruité, du soleil, du

ERNESTINES

Pâte d'amandes et zeste de citron

Tout moelleux, tout gentil !

CALISSONS CLASSIQUES

Amande, orange confite

Allez-y, comparez !

FEUILLES DE HOUX

Sésame

Si, si, la graine de sésame peut avoir du goût, la preuve …

NOUGAT AUX AMANDES

garanties de Provence, les amandes

celui que tout le monde fait avec plus ou moins de bonheur …

NOUGAT AUX PIGNONS

de nos jours, garantis du Portugal, mais la Provence en produisait …

splendeur d'un fruit mythique

Pine nuts and Honey Nougat

5 euro

NOUGAT AUX PIGNONS

…es du Portugal, les pignons de pin

…l Provence en a eu produit

…deur d'un fruit mythique

amandes de Provence, un rien de safran

tour de magie du XIIIème siècle :

où est donc passé le goût du sucre ?

Almonds and Honey without sugar taste

5 euro

Orielle de la Bonne Déesse

Le Petit Duc

OREILLES DE LA BONNE DÉESSE

La Méditerranée en une bouchée !
À tremper dans du vin rouge uniquement !
Ni thé, ni café !
All the roman civilisation in one bit …

sachet	3 euros
ruche orange	6 euros
petite rectangulaire	9 euros

AU PETIT DUC

Bread
Jean Luc Poujauran

Jean Luc Poujauran's story is a modern-day tale of greed, jealousy and mad inventors. In 2003, Poujauran had been making his fabulous bread in his beautiful baker's shop, set practically in the shadow of the Eiffel Tower on rue Jean Nicot in the 7th arrondissement, for 27 years. Faithful clients would cross Paris for his moist, light, rich yeasty bread, made only from the finest flour, generous amounts of natural yeast, organic salt from Guérande and purified water. Poujauran also perfected a double fermentation in the baking process, adding extra air and flavour to his loaves.

After a contractural disagreement with his ex-partner, Jean Luc found himself doing business next door to a bakery selling bread made by someone else but sold under the Poujauran name. The strict 'law of disloyal competition' in France meant that Poujauran could not sell his bread to the public with his own name in the same street as his ex-partner, who now held the rights to his ex-bakery and continued to call it 'Pain Poujauran'.

Poujauran couldn't just up and leave, he had heavily invested in the business. So he 'took his courage in two hands' as the French say, and, literally, dug in next to his now sworn enemy. For although he had lost his shop and most of the baking equipment, he owned the old chemist's shop next door, and, more importantly, its cellars. With the help of a team of canny Portuguese builders who were familiar with the labyrinths of cellars and tunnels in Paris, they tunnelled under the floors and, secretly, bucket by bucket, dug out a new space into which Poujauran installed his newly invented, revolutionary bread-making machines and bread ovens.

Obsessed with reducing the number of times the dough was manipulated by hand, in order to minimise loss of air and texture in the bread, he designed machines that move, weigh and cut the dough automatically. Where hands cannot be replaced is in the kneading and shaping of the loaves. From 1am onwards, five bakers work through the night preparing orders for the following morning.

Now Poujauran's bread is available in Paris's best restaurants and through several gourmet outlets, including an internet delivery service called 'Le Haut du Panier', created with two celebrity supplier friends, Joel Thiebault, a vegetable grower, and Philippe Aléosse, the cheese seller.

He was the first Parisian baker to serve *canelés* – little flowerpot-shaped caramelised crêpe cakes from the Bordeaux region, now furiously fashionable all over France. His *Galette des Rois* is also legendary. Traditionally served at Epiphany, galettes start appearing in shops around Christmas but exit fast after the official date as it is considered bad luck to eat them any later. The galette is a closed tart made from almond paste-filled puff pastry, glazed with butter and usually served warm. Inside is hidden a *fève* (lucky charm). Originally a dried bean, now they take all sorts of shapes. Jean Luc's are copies of his favourite vintage delivery van! His galette is sold at a few select restaurants and Paris's famous concept store, Colette.

The new Primitive Arts Museum in Quai Branly now has its own Pain Poujauran, made with flax seed, barley and oat flour.

But he bitterly misses his old customers, and they miss him. Some say that Catherine Deneuve and Isabelle Adjani have been spotted coming secretly, crossing the little court-yard next to the underground bakery, when the desire for a Poujauran fix becomes just too much for them.

chapter 2
knows her classics

The French home cook knows her classics. By that I am not saying she
can whirl into her kitchen and produce every one of the recipes in this
chapter without glancing at a cookery book or ruffling her chignon.
But, unlike all but the most informed foodie in Britain, she will know
of and about almost all the dishes and will be intensely aware and
proud of their Frenchness, for they are all around her, in some form or
another, and always have been.

These dishes are the *plat du jour* at the bistro she passes by on her way to work; their three-starred re-interpretation by a famous chef has been reported in this morning's Figaro newspaper; her grandmother used to cook most of them, and her mother complained about having to do just that; her best friend proudly produced 'her version' at the dinner party she held last night, and chances are it will be the main subject of conversation next time they meet.

As she shops she can buy classic dishes pre-prepared in the supermarket, at the frozen-food counter or at the *traiteur*. If she is going to cook one herself, she can pick up the recipe as she buys its ingredients, just by asking a shopkeeper, or even someone in the queue. Alternatively, bookshops and hypermarkets are full of cookery books from the most basic to those by superstar chef Alain Ducasse, or she can choose one from the twenty or so food magazines on offer at the newsagents.

Food blogs are developing fast. The first were very much English/American expat foodie newsletters, helping to stave off homesickness by sharing information about where to find Philly cheese for a real cheesecake or the hottest new bistro. But now French writers and culinary creators are using them to build networks linking restaurants, PR, publishing and journalism.

The French feminist movement's achievements came very late compared to those in the UK. Feminist attitudes to cooking as drudgery meant that mother-to-daughter teaching didn't happen for a whole generation. The way the French home cook has learned her classics has changed and why she would want to learn has changed even more. Now cooking is becoming sexy again, with the embracing of more *bobo* (bourgeois–bohemian) values. The daughters of rebellious *soixante-huitardes* (the generation involved in the strikes and student demos of 1968) are rebelling in turn against their mothers' intellectual anti-gourmet, dismal culinary performances and turning cooking into a means of expression as personalised as what they wear or how they decorate their homes.

As lifestyles change radically, French home cooks may have become more negligent about traditional gastronomy, but they still have it in their bones. Cooking styles are becoming more polarised. Weekday sustenance is thrown into contrast with the marathons of weekend cooking as leisure and cultural activity. Local, countryside foods and regional cuisines are experiencing a strong revival as dishes for entertaining. Recipes for *baeckhoffe* from Alsace, *poulet Vallée d'Auge* from Normandy, and *grand aïoli* from Marseilles are being dusted off and cooked as often as time allows their now perceived-as-pleasurable preparation.

Even in the provinces, where classic French dishes are cooked much more often as a matter of course than in Paris, two-hour lunch breaks are dwindling and what used to be the main family meal of the day is taken more and more often at the 'self' (self-service cafeteria), the canteen or the salad and sandwich bar. Evening meals are cooked more quickly, and the plancha, the wok and the barbecue are creeping into more and more homes as cooking in fat, be it butter or olive oil, gets pushed aside for more healthy and rapid alternatives to a four-hour bourguignon. But the French are still cooking from scratch all the time. At the supermarkets, processed and pre-assembled dishes are still shunned in favour of loose ingredients that will be transformed into dishes, even if they are less complex, time-consuming and traditionally French. The evening meal is still an occasion. Very often it will be light: soup, quiche, cold or grilled meat or fish served with salad or vegetables. Cheese and fruit are ubiquitous, and desserts are reserved for entertaining or weekends. It is prepared more quickly, goes by faster, but the time slot has changed little. Everyone sits down around 8pm, explaining why club (and pub!) life is so confined to weekends and why more thought is naturally put into what will be on the table.

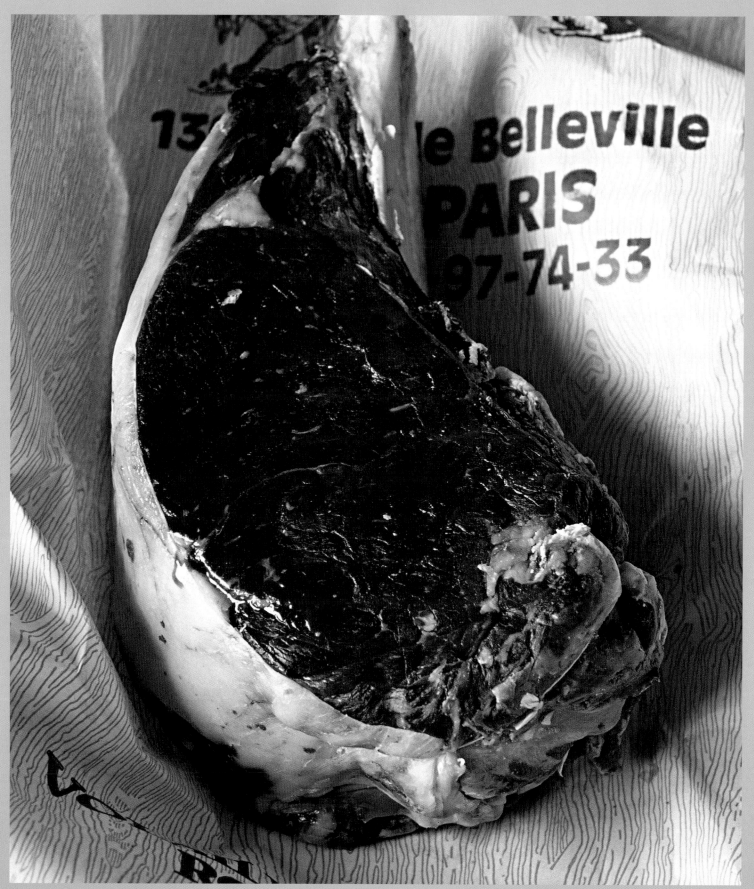

old faithfuls

a good steak

It is as subjective a concept as a good cup of tea, with as many cultural variations. The Americans think the French don't understand that good means thick. For the British, good means cooked. Countless times I have found myself apologising to French waiters when accompanied by my children or Irish visitors who ask for their steak *bien cuit*, to ensure they will be served. Once, in a starry restaurant, the waiter refused to take the order for a well-done steak. He demanded that my baffled Scottish friend choose another dish, rather than 'wasting' a good piece of meat on a philistine who didn't like the taste of blood.

An advantage of toeing the French line of thinner-cut steaks, cooked rare, is that the cooking technique is very simple. The pan, grill or barbecue must be piping hot and stay that way throughout cooking. Fat (clarified butter, animal fat or oil) is used sparingly, if at all, and cooking time kept to a minimum in order to achieve the contrast between seared outer crust and tender inner pinkness.

An exception on the thickness front is the majestic *côte de boeuf* (see photograph left). Best cooked on a charcoal barbecue, rested a full 10 minutes then sliced up and served in rectangular, thin tranches, it will take a little longer but will nevertheless be served bloody in the middle. It is vital that the beef be at room temperature when it reaches the coals otherwise the outside will be blackened by the time the inside warms up.

... with real chips

The writer Maurice Edmond Sailland, great defender of French cuisine, humbly declared in 1927, 'Chips are one of the most spiritual creations of Parisian genius' and further fuelled a Franco-Belgian debate centuries old and hotter than the heart of a deep-fat fryer. With such an acknowledged wealth of culinary history, the French could give up claiming they invented every recipe in the world, especially for a dish as unrepresentative of fine French cooking as the mere chip.

The Belgians say the first mention of *pommes frites* was made in a manuscript dated 1781, describing how the inhabitants of Wallonie, faced with a frozen river Meuse, substituted potatoes cut into fish shapes for the real things they loved to deep-fry in beef fat. The French, naturally rather more grandly, say the *pommes Pont Neuf* were yet another fabulous innovation born out of the revolution.

Once pedigree is established, and a consensus reached regarding which varieties of potato to use (King Edward, Maris Piper or Désirée), the discussion can progress to which fat is used to fry them in. My personal favourite is goose fat. Any animal fat — beef, lamb, pork or even horse (Terence Conran's preference) — will give you that artery-blocking authentic taste. Groundnut or sunflower oil are the most popular choice for a healthier chip you will then eat more of.

The most important tricks lie in the preparation. Wiping off excess starch from freshly cut chips and twicefold cooking, draining and increasing the temperature between bubbling baths, will give fantastically crisp yet fondant fries.

Heat the fat to 160°C/325°F.

Peel the potatoes (2 per person), then wash them clean of any dirt. Cut them into 1cm slices, then cut the slices into chip shapes. Wipe the chips with a tea-towel, but don't dry them out completely.

In batches to suit your fryer, put the chips into the frying basket and lower into the fat, shaking carefully and regularly as they cook to avoid them sticking together, and let them cook for about 10 minutes. The chips should be cooked through and moist right to the centre.

Remove the basket of chips and let them drain as you heat the fat to 190°C/375°F. Then give them a quick 2–3 minutes more in the fryer until they are delectably golden.

Turn them out onto some kitchen paper to drain off excess fat, then put them on plates or in a serving dish and sprinkle with some fleur de sel (sea salt), and pepper if that's the way you like them.

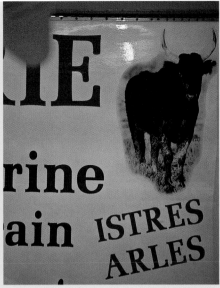

Steak tartare

A classic *brasserie* dish, steak tartare's theatrical preparation at the table by your solemn, long-aproned, curly-moustached waiter will be half its appeal. Tradition has it that horse meat is the best choice for a good French tartare. This is perhaps a nod to the Mongolian origin of the dish: on the warpath Tatars reportedly carried raw meat under their saddles, making it as tender and instantly available as a Big Mac. As with the omelette, when serving a tartare, individual preferences are sacred – I love chopping oysters into mine.

FOR 4

800 g – 1 kg finest sirloin steak
4 very, very fresh eggs
3 medium onions, finely chopped
Tabasco
Worcestershire sauce
Extra virgin olive oil
Fleur de sel (sea salt)
Freshly ground black pepper

FOR THE MIXING INGREDIENTS
4 tablespoons drained capers
4 tablespoons chopped cornichons
4 tablespoons Dijon mustard
4 tablespoons ketchup
4 tablespoons chopped flat-leaf
  parsley

An hour or so before serving, chop the steak finely with a very sharp knife, cover with clingfilm and refrigerate.

Just before serving, divide the meat into four and arrange in a neat circle, square or oblong on each plate.

Separate the eggs. Make a little well in each tartare and place an egg yolk in the centre. I like presenting the yolks in a half eggshell, although this apparently heightens even more the chances of bacterial attacks. If you are rigorous about using very fresh eggs this shouldn't be a problem.

Set small piles of all the mixing ingredients around the meat, put sauce bottles and salt and pepper on the table (preferring perhaps a just-opened, cult-status glass bottle of Heinz ketchup to the half-finished, family-size, plastic Tesco's easy-squeeze) and serve with a crunchy green salad and real chips.

Salade niçoise

This is surely the most famous and argued-over salad in the world. The purists banish lettuce and any boiled vegetables, and swear by cucumbers, fresh basil, little violet artichokes and *fèves* (beans). Just tell yourself that if you are not from Nice, you can never get it right, and go where your taste takes you. Personally, over the years I have got used to the soft blandness boiled potatoes give in contrast to the green-bean crunch and saltiness from olives and anchovies, and am pretty loath to give them up. In this version I have sacrilegiously seared the tuna and kept everything mini, to vary proportions rather than taste.

FOR 4

200g tuna, good-quality tinned or fresh from a fillet for searing

4 whole anchovy fillets in olive oil

8 quail's eggs, or 2 hen's eggs, hard-boiled and halved

8 ripe cherry tomatoes, halved

A good handful of black olives (ideally French, from Nice even better)

4 medium potatoes, boiled and cooled, then sliced

A good handful of green beans, lightly boiled or steamed to give a nice crunch

¹/₂ red pepper, sliced

¹/₂ yellow pepper, sliced

FOR THE DRESSING

4 tablespoons extra virgin olive oil

1 garlic clove, crushed

Fleur de sel (sea salt)

Freshly ground black pepper

If using fresh tuna, heat a little olive oil in a very hot pan and sear the tuna quickly on all sides to form a pale crust. Leave to cool, then slice the fish very thinly.

Combine all the ingredients in a salad bowl or line them up for a more graphic effect (only if you haven't invited any French guests).

For the dressing, mix the the olive oil with the garlic, season and serve with the salad.

the real niçoise from a real Niçoise

If you wanted to be authentic, you would combine 10 medium tomatoes (cut into quarters), 1 cucumber (peeled and chopped), 200g raw fresh fève beans, 12 small violet artichokes (but not those from Brittany), raw and sliced, 2 green peppers, deseeded and chopped, 6 basil leaves, 3 hard-boiled eggs (cut in half), 12 anchovy fillets, 300g good-quality tinned tuna in brine, 100g black niçoise olives in a bowl, season with salt and pepper and mix with olive oil and crushed garlic.

Soupe à l'oignon   Onion soup

Originally from Lyons, onion soup was made popular during the nineteenth century by Parisan market workers in Les Halles. Traditionally served after a *nuit blanche* (sleepless night) because of its supposed ability to quickly dissipate the effects of alcohol, it is an invigorating and revitalising soup.

FOR 4

150 g butter

4 medium–large onions, sliced

1 garlic clove, crushed

100 ml red wine

150 ml beef stock

Sprig of thyme

2 bay leaves

1 baguette

150 g grated gruyère cheese

Heat the butter in a large, deep, heavy-based saucepan. Gently fry the onion and garlic for about 15 minutes. They must be soft, brown and lightly caramelised. Be careful not to let them fry crisp.

Add the wine, stock, thyme and bay leaves. Bring to the boil, then reduce the heat and simmer very gently for around 30 minutes, stirring from time to time.

Preheat the grill. Cut the baguette into 2 cm slices and toast it on both sides.

Pour the soup into ovenproof bowls, place 1 or 2 pieces of baguette on top and sprinkle generously with the grated gruyère. Put the bowls under the hot grill.

When the cheese is golden and bubbling, remove from the oven and serve immediately.

Omelette

Volumes have been written about whether you should frittata, flip or fold. The classic French omelette is folded into an oval shape, pale on the outside, wet on the inside, and served with a simple green salad and bread. Much of how it turns out depends more on wrist action during the egg-beating than recipe proportions or additions. Personal variations have been encouraged since Auguste Escoffier, the turn-of-the-century 'king of chefs and chef of kings' declared that omelette should always be cooked to each guest's preference. My eldest son, although not keen on desserts, has his sprinkled with sugar. World leaders and film stars eat theirs foamy and enormous at La Mère Poularde on the Mont Saint Michel.

We are not crazy about omelettes in my house but eggs, be they scrambled, boiled or poached, are a wonderful base for other flavours. With such a pure canvas, I like to keep things really simple. Chives, tarragon and chervil are very good sprinkled into the beaten eggs before cooking. Sometimes I'll add some cream or milk. Grated parmesan and cheddar toast nicely on the surface. Crumbled feta or goat's cheese will stay soft and give a bit of tang. Truffles, black and white, love landing in this eggy cushion.

FOR 1

3 eggs, organic if possible
Vegetable oil, for frying
Unsalted butter
Salt and freshly ground black pepper

Break the eggs into a bowl and beat them lightly with a fork.

Briskly heat a little oil and a knob of butter in a heavy-based pan or omelette pan. When they are sizzling ('singing', the French say) pour in the eggs and stir lightly with the fork until they are cooked (but not browned) underneath and still runny on top.

Fold a third of the omelette over towards the middle, then fold over the opposite third to form an oval shape.

Slide the omelette out of the pan. Season with salt and pepper and serve.

Frisée aux lardons

Bacon and poached egg salad

As with many classic French salads, there are a few hotly disputed versions in circulation. Eggs and croûtons don't seem to cohabit well and I always prefer mopping up the egg yolk with fluffy baguette to chasing it around with fried cubes, however crunchy and garlicky they may be.

FOR 4

5 tablespoons extra virgin olive oil

2 tablespoons wine vinegar

1 teaspoon Dijon mustard

250 g lardons or a slice of *poitrine fumée* (thick-cut smoked bacon) cut into 2 cm lardons

4 eggs

1 frisée salad, washed, spun, leaves detached and torn into manageable pieces

Salt and freshly ground black pepper

Make a vinaigrette by combining the oil, vinegar and mustard. Season lightly as the *poitrine* is very salty.

Fry the *poitrine* in a pan until golden and crispy. No need to add oil or butter! Meanwhile lightly poach the eggs.

Put the prepared frisée in a salad bowl and toss it with the dressing. Sprinkle on the lardons (avoid pouring in the fat from the pan!) and serve, setting the eggs on top.

Croque monsieur ou madame

FOR 4

8 slices white bread

4 slices ham

100 g grated gruyère cheese

4 eggs or not, depending on croque gender

Salt and freshly ground black pepper

FOR THE BECHAMEL SAUCE

30 g butter

2 tablespoons plain flour

300 ml milk

30 g grated gruyère cheese

Pinch of ground nutmeg

Preheat the grill.

To make the béchamel sauce, melt the butter in a saucepan and sprinkle the flour on top. Stir into a paste with a wooden spoon and cook very gently for 2 minutes.

Add the milk, using a whisk if lumps form, and heat gently until it comes to the boil, then simmer very gently, stirring constantly. Add the cheese and nutmeg as the sauce thickens. Take it off the heat when it is thick and set aside.

Spread some béchamel on 4 slices of bread and set a slice of ham on each. Take half the 100 g of grated gruyère and sprinkle it over the ham. Top with a second slice of bread, and spread some béchamel and the rest of the gruyère on each. Cook under the grill for 3–4 minutes until the cheese is golden and bubbling.

If you want a Croque Madame, fry the eggs while the sandwiches are under the grill then pop them on top. Served with a green salad and some tomatoes, the Croque *Couple* is still a popular (and balanced) dish for a family evening meal.

Pot au feu

The *pot au feu* has been simmering beside French fires and atop stoves for centuries. Essentially a beef and vegetable stew, traditionally served in two stages: first as soup, a dark and flavoursome consommé; and then as a hearty dish of boiled beef with poached vegetables accompanied sometimes by a marrow bone with croûtons. French mustard, *gros sel* (cooking or coarse sea salt) and cornichons are the traditional condiments.

Threatened with extinction by the 21st-century lifestyle, which is incompatible with skimming and adding vegetables to a simmering pot for four hours, as *bistro* cooking and now *cuisine bourgeoise* come back into fashion, *pot au feu* is now increasingly popular for entertaining, despite the time involved. It benefits from being made the day before, and it's a comforting, healthy dish that everyone loves, providing starter and main course in one. More creative French cooks vary the meat, from beef cheeks and oxtail to duck and foie gras, and flavour the broth with spices and herbs, producing sophisticated versions a far cry from the 18th-century staple.

In Paris, rue de Vignon near Place de La Madeleine, the famous bistro Le Roi du Pot au Feu serves, non stop, a consummate *pot au feu* which has inspired this recipe.

FOR 4

1.5 kg rib, shoulder or leg of beef
  (ask your butcher to tie the meat
  with string)
1 bouquet garni
300 g carrots, cut in 4–6 cm pieces,
  and halved if they are very thick
200 g turnips, peeled but left whole
  if they are the size of medium
  potatoes, cut into chunks if very big
2 onions, skins on, studded with cloves
2 large leeks, or 3 medium ones,
  green tops removed
About 12 medium potatoes,
  peeled but left whole
4 marrow bones, 3 cm long (optional)
French mustard and cornichons,
  to serve
Salt

Fill a very large stockpot half full with cold water. Add the meat and a tablespoon of salt and bring slowly to the boil.

Add 100 ml of cold water and, with a slotted spoon, skim off the scum and fat on the surface and return to the boil. Repeat the process two or three times. The more you do it, the clearer and lighter the *bouillon* (stock) will be.

Add the bouquet garni and all the vegetables except for the potatoes, and leave to simmer very gently, uncovered, for 4 hours, skimming off scum and fat as often as you can.

About 45 minutes before serving, boil the potatoes in a separate pan and set aside. If you want an immaculately limpid soup, remove the meat and vegetables from the stock, keep them warm and strain the stock through a muslin cloth.

If you are serving marrow bones, poach them for 3–5 minutes very, very gently in a saucepan of barely simmering, salted water until they are soft. You could also roast them in a hot oven for a five minutes or until they start to bubble.

Serve the *bouillon* in soup bowls, then, in large, deep dishes serve the meat, vegetables and marrow bones, with a little *bouillon* poured over, accompanied by mustard, cornichons and *gros sel*.

(At the Roi du Pot au Feu, the marrow bones are served as a starter with toasted baguette and *gros sel* – as delicate and rich as the finest foie gras).

Poulet Vallée d'Auge

Chicken with cream, apples and mushrooms

The Vallée d'Auge in Normandy is a green, lush region famous for its cream, cheese and apples. This is the type of rich, pre-nouvelle cuisine dish that gives French cooking a bad name but that everyone secretly adores: cream, wine, chicken and mushrooms must be the most has-been but heavenly combo in all of French cuisine.

It is the first recipe I ever cooked for a dinner party, from the first cookery book I owned, *French Cooking* by Elisabeth Scotto. I 'checked the seasoning' so often as I was cooking it that I had to dash out at 6 o'clock to buy more of everything.

FOR 6

2 tablespoons olive oil

75 g butter

2 onions, finely chopped

6 chicken pieces (breasts, thighs or legs, or a mix of pieces)

A small glass of Calvados (optional)

500 ml dry cider

500 g button mushrooms, finely sliced

500 ml double cream or crème fraîche

Salt and freshly ground black pepper

In a heavy-based saucepan with a lid, heat the olive oil with half the butter. Add the chopped onion and the chicken pieces, browning them all over.

Pour in the Calvados, if using, stir well, rubbing at the hardened cooking juices stuck on the pan to deglaze. If you like, ignite the alcohol to flambé the dish – and be careful you don't inadvertently flambé your eyebrows if you are working on a gas flame. If that all sounds too scary, or if you don't have any Calvados, leaving out this step won't spoil the dish.

Add the cider, again scratching around the bottom of the pan to get at all the flavoursome caramelised bits, and bring to a slow simmer.

In a separate pan, heat the rest of the butter and fry the mushrooms until they render their juice.

Add them to the chicken, season very lightly and cook together for around 30 minutes. I don't pour all the mushroom juices in as I find it makes the sauce too runny. But their taste is good.

Add the cream and cook for a further 10 minutes or so. Season to taste.

If the sauce is sufficiently thick, adjust the seasoning and serve the dish like this. Alternatively, you can spoon out the chicken and most of the mushrooms, keep them warm and reduce the sauce further by simmering it on its own for a while.

An appropriately Norman accompaniment would be *pommes en l'air* (apples peeled, cut in slices or quarters, and gently fried in butter). Fresh pasta or boiled potatoes are fine as well.

Canard à l'orange

Duck à l'orange

There are many versions of this festive dish and, for once, there is very little preaching about which is the real thing. The duck should be roasted or pot-roasted and its cooking juices then mixed with orangey additions to make a rich sauce. This version is as uncomplicated as it is decadent, for even though the rather retro Grand Marnier or Cointreau are left out, the sauce starts with caramel and is finished off with butter.

When I first made this dish, I was thrown by the amount of very runny orange sauce that had been produced. In full view of my mother-in-law, I did as I had been taught in County Antrim and reached for the Bisto tin. For her, it was a wildy exotic and revolutionary addition and she begged me to bring her some back from my next visit home to Ireland.

Thankfully the whole thing was delicious and, as usual, my miscalculation was treated with mildly patronising amusement. Luckily my Irish roots also had me cooking too many potatoes, so with all that gorgeous sauce to soak up no one was left hungry. I only realised retrospectively, when I ran out of Bisto, how tragically overpowered the ducky orange taste had been.

FOR 4

2 carrots, cut into 2cm chunks

2 shallots, cut into quarters

1 bay leaf

1 orange, unwaxed, cut into quarters

1 duck, about 1.5–1.75kg, ready for the oven: washed, dried, rubbed with salt and pepper and anointed with olive oil

100g sugar

Zest of 2 oranges

250ml freshly squeezed orange juice

75g butter (approximately, but let greed be your guide)

1 orange, unwaxed, unpeeled and finely sliced

Salt and freshly ground black pepper

Preheat the oven to 180°C/350°F/gas mark 4.

Put the carrots, most of the shallots, the bay leaf and half the orange quarters into a roasting tin. Squeeze the orange quarters a little to release some juice.

Put the remaining shallot and orange quarters inside the duck's cavity, set it on the vegetables and roast for about 1 hour 15 minutes, basting as often as you can – every 30 minutes would be ideal.

Remove the duck from the oven, pour off the meat cooking juices into a bowl, then keep the duck warm. If you feel like it, press the cooking vegetables through a conic sieve to extract all the flavour from them into the juices, then discard the sieve contents.

Put the sugar into a medium heavy-based saucepan and add 2 tablespoons water. Heat it slowly, turning the pan but not stirring with a spoon (otherwise crystals, then lumps, will form), until it becomes a syrup. Let this bubble for about $1^{1}/_{2}$-2 minutes until it starts to caramelise. When it is a dark golden colour, take it off the heat and gently add the duck cooking juices, the orange zest and juice. Be careful the caramel doesn't spit and burn you.

Put the pan back on the heat and simmer for about 15 minutes to reduce the sauce, then season with salt and pepper. Whisk the butter into the sauce, add the orange slices and let them heat through.

Bring the duck to the table and carve it there – it's very easy and won't take long as there are only four pieces to dislodge. Serve with boiled new potatoes and baby carrots.

Gigot d'agneau à la cuillère

Roast lamb served with a spoon

I will always remember the first time I encountered this fabulous slow-cooked dish. It was made by an inspirational cook, my beloved aunt-in-law, Odile, at some important gathering of my ultra-traditional *belle-famille*. The only equipment she had in her tiny cottage was one of those mini-ovens that claimed to do everything splendidly but in reality did nothing properly. For once the fact that she could never get it to heat up decently played in her favour, or so she thought.

There was complete silence as the lamb was spooned onto plates.

My father-in-law went pale at the sight of no blood. You see, he reared sheep, in a 'weekend and after-work, Marie Antoinette-meets-Gordon Ramsay pseudo rustic' way, and was used to eating his lamb practically tripping off the carving board, almost disappointed at a lack of visible pulse when he cut into it. His brother-in-law seemed to instantly regret opening the magnum of Château Margaux he had brought along. Odile's father-in-law (my grandfather-in-law, at the time a pernickety 92 year old), who should have listened to his probably rejoicing teeth, ungraciously pronounced the melting, intensely flavoured dish 'a waste of good meat' and Odile looked as if she would cry. Naturally, any consolation from her beef-boiling-Brit of a *belle-nièce* (niece-in-law) was of no value whatsoever.

Of course had we all been Alsatians, the reaction would have been very different. In Alsace, slow-cooking is a very popular method of getting the most flavour out of meat. *Gigot à la cuillère* is often served there. The regional dish *baeckhoffe*, a layered stew not unlike a Lancashire hotpot, takes its name from the enormous clay dish in which it is cooked. In the past, the ingenious, multi-tasking women of villages in Alsace would be allowed to pop their pots of meat and vegetables into the baker's oven, still warm from making the morning batch of bread, on their way to the *lavoir* (wash-house) or the fields. They would pick them up for the evening meal as they returned from a hard day's work, content in the knowledge they could put a hot meal on the table for man and children. We can take a leaf out of their books (though overnight cooking in our own ovens would be more prudent than asking to squat the local baker's or leaving ours on all day in an empty house).

This dish requires seven hours of cooking in the oven. It also calls for browning the meat, then transferring it to a large casserole dish for slow cooking. You could be lazier, and do the browning in the casserole and then simply deglaze with the wine as with many bourguignon-type stews. But this dish has a gentler, more aromatic personality than robustly braised beef and it really is best to get rid of any bitter burned bits which could permeate through the finished dish.

FOR 6

1 leg of lamb, 2–2.5 kg (ask your butcher to bone, roll and tie it if possible; if it's on the bone, don't despair, but you may need a bigger cooking pot)
8–10 garlic cloves, halved
2–3 tablespoons olive oil
3 large onions, coarsely chopped
8 shallots, coarsely chopped
3 carrots, cut into large chunks
1 celery stick, cut into large chunks
Fresh rosemary and thyme
3–4 bay leaves
8–10 juniper berries
1 small glass cognac (optional)
1 litre dry white wine
Salt and freshly ground pepper

Preheat the oven to 150°C/300°F/gas mark 2.

Make lots of tiny incisions into the lamb and insert the half-cloves of garlic.

Heat the oil in a large heavy-based frying pan or saucepan and brown the lamb all over. Add the onions, shallots, carrots and celery and give it all a bit of a fry and stir. (If you can't fit all the vegetables in the pan, don't worry, you can add them to the casserole dish afterwards.)

Transfer the lamb and the vegetables to a large casserole dish with a lid, discarding any burned residue but keeping the other cooking juices and fat. Add the herbs and the juniper berries.

If you like, flambé the lamb – it's not vital, but it does add an even more luxurious depth of flavour to the final result. Heat the cognac in a separate saucepan, pour it onto the lamb and set it alight. Let the flames die down before proceeding to the next stage.

Pour in the wine, season lightly and bring to the boil.

Put the lid on, transfer to the oven and cook for about 7 hours, checking from time to time and adding water or chicken stock if it seems to be drying out too quickly.

Serve with creamy potato gratin or garlic mash, and perhaps some crunchy green beans or sugar snaps.

Boeuf bourguignon

This is one of France's most famous and best-loved dishes: a rich and hearty stew, whose flavour becomes even better when it is reheated the next day. This is another recipe I learnt from Elizabeth Scotto.

FOR 4–6

1 large onion, chopped
Sprig flat-leaf parsley
Sprig of thyme
1 bay leaf
1.5 kg chuck steak or top rump,
   cut into large chunks
2 tablespoons cognac
500 ml red wine
4–5 tablespoons olive oil
50 g butter
150 g *poitrine fumée* (bacon lardons)
24 small pickling onions
450 g button mushrooms, sliced
25 g plain flour
400 ml beef stock
1 garlic clove, crushed

In a deep bowl, put a few of the onion slices, some parsley, thyme and the bay leaf. Add a few pieces of beef on top, then layer up until all the beef, parsley and thyme are used up.

Mix together the cognac, wine and 3 tablespoons of oil, and pour them over the beef. Cover the bowl with clingfilm and refrigerate for at least 4 hours, stirring occasionally.

In a large frying pan, heat the butter and fry the *poitrine fumée* with the pickling onions and the mushrooms until they become golden. Drain on some kitchen paper and set aside.

Put the flour on a plate. Drain the beef, reserving the marinade, and dry with kitchen paper.

In a heavy-based casserole dish with a lid, heat the remaining oil. Roll the beef quickly in the flour and brown in the hot fat for a few minutes until lightly coloured all over. Sprinkle in any remaining flour and cook for a further 1–2 minutes. Stir.

Pour in the marinade, stirring and scraping off any tasty bits stuck to the bottom of the pan. Cover and simmer very gently for about 2 hours.

Add the *poitrine fumée*, mushrooms and pickling onions and cook for a further 30 minutes or until the beef is meltingly tender.

Terrine de poisson   Fish terrine

Cold fish-based terrines are the centrepieces of many buffet tables at summer get-togethers. Everybody's mother-in-law seems to have her own recipe, from the simple salmon version below to elaborate three-tiered constructions.

FOR 6

Butter, for greasing
12 eggs
100 ml single cream
100 ml double cream
500 g cooked mixed vegetables,
   such as peas, green beans,
   courgettes, carrots and asparagus
2–3 tablespoons chopped fresh herbs,
   such as basil, chives, chervil and dill
400 g salmon fillets, skin removed

Preheat the oven to 200°C/400°F/gas mark 6. Use the butter to grease a 22cm cake tin.

In a large bowl, beat the eggs with the creams. Mix in the vegetables and the herbs. Season well with salt and freshly ground black pepper.

Pour half the vegetable mixture into the prepared cake tin. Lay the salmon on it, filling in the gaps around the side of the tin. Then pour the remaining vegetable mixture on top.

Place the cake tin in a roasting tin or large gratin dish and pour enough warm water around the cake tin for it to be half immersed (this is a bain-marie). Cook in the oven for about 1 hour.

Remove from the oven. Cover with foil and leave to cool, then chill in the fridge for 2–3 hours. Serve with a herb and/or lemon-flavoured light mayonnaise, 'mousseline', or a tomato coulis.

Sole meunière

Ordering sole meunière is a restaurant critic's infallible method of testing the quality of the service, the produce and the way it is cooked, because in theory it's such a simple dish, but in practice so often massacred. At home, there are three important things to know when aiming for the perfect moist yet crispy sole: first, use the freshest fish you can find; second, always add a little oil to the butter in the pan to prevent it from burning; and third, make sure this is nice and hot before you dust the fish with flour, otherwise the flour will soak up moisture from the flesh and form soggy clumps when it hits the pan.

FOR 4

4 soles around 200–250 g each,
   skinned and gutted by your
   fishmonger
2–3 tablespoons plain flour
200 g butter, plus 200 g for melting
   and pouring
2 tablespoons sunflower oil
1 lemon, quartered
Salt and freshly ground black pepper

Rinse the fish under cold running water, then pat it dry with kitchen paper.

Spread out the flour on a large flat plate and season with salt and pepper.

In a large frying pan (if you don't own a large enough pan, you may have to cook the fish one at a time) heat 50 g of butter per fish with half a tablespoon of oil until they begin to sizzle and foam.

Press both sides of the fish quickly into the flour. Brush and shake off the excess flour and drop the fish immediately into the pan.

Cook the fish for 5 minutes each side on a medium heat. Remove it from the pan, squeeze over a little lemon juice and keep it warm in the oven. Repeat with the rest of the fish.

Quickly clean and dry the pan. Heat the remaining 200 g of butter until it turns nut-brown. Pour it over the fish.

Moules marinière

This can be a very communal dish. There is a camaraderie attached to eating *moules frites*, mussels steamed in wine and herbs and served with chips. At the Braderie de Lille, a huge seven-day autumn flea market that invades the entire city and is France's largest public gathering, over 500 tonnes of mussels are consumed. Their empty shells are piled up on the pavement in front of each restaurant, in a competition to find out which place was most popular with hungry visitors.

At home, mussels are often pre-announced to guests as the *raison d'être* of the evening. 'Come tonight, I'm cooking *moules frites*' your host will say. And, just as with *raclette* or *crêpes* or a leg of wild boar, or a *pot au feu*, the gathering is defined and justified by the food being served. Rejoicing in and sharing it is the only goal.

My children love mussels. It's an attraction–repulsion thing, something I have exploited over and over to get them to try things: it starts as a 'bet you won't eat that' challenge and then, miraculously, they discover they love the taste. They also love the way you can use one empty hinged shell to pinch out the next mussel, the fact that there are often little hitchhiker crabs hiding inside and the way each empty shell can be neatly slotted into the next one, bending a shiny, black purple garland around their plates.

FOR 4

2 kg mussels (avoid the pre-cleaned
    and pre-packed, and buy them
    as fresh as you can. In France,
    choose 'bouchot', the best, grown
    on wooden posts)
50 g butter
2 tablespoons sunflower oil
1 garlic clove, finely chopped
2–3 shallots, finely chopped
A good handful of curly parsley,
    finely chopped
2–3 glasses dry white wine
Freshly ground black pepper

Clean the mussels: under cold running water, scrub them and pull off the gritty beards. Discard any that are open and do not close as you press on them.

In a very large, deep saucepan, heat the butter with the oil and gently sweat the garlic and shallots. Add the parsley, white wine and some pepper and bring to the boil.

Throw in the mussels, put the lid on and cook for 2–3 minutes. Give the pan a shake or dig down to the bottom once or twice with a ladle to make sure they cook evenly. The mussels are cooked when the shells are open and the flesh is tender.

Discard any mussels that have remained closed, then with a large slotted spoon transfer the mussels to deep plates. Ladle the glorious cooking liquid over them and serve.

Other tasty possibilities are cooking the mussels in pastis instead of wine, or, for *moules à la crème*, adding a few tablespoons of crème fraîche to the cooking liquid after the mussels are cooked.

Le grand aïoli

There is something addictive about tongue-burningly fresh, raw garlic. When you spend time in the south of France in summer, lazily adjusting to the heat and incumbent slowness of life that make time itself so hazy, you soon begin to crave it at every meal. Suddenly you find yourself adding it to sweet fresh tomato paste on toasted baguette for breakfast as fear of the inevitable consequences fades, just as with any other addictive substance. In Provence, the famously welcoming locals joke about how tourists react so badly to garlic they are more identifiable by their new *parfum* than their Minoltas and badly cut Bermudas.

Aïoli is a strong garlic mayonnaise and, by extension the name of the famous Provençal dish with which it is served. Frédéric Mistral, the poet largely responsible for the revival of the Occitan language in the late 19th century, wrote: 'It intoxicates gently, fills the body with warmth, and the soul with enthusiasm. In its essence it concentrates the strength, the gaiety of Provence: sunshine.'

The sauce ignites and unites the more delicate flavours of other *Grand Aïoli* ingredients: an array of poached or steamed vegetables, poached salt cod, hard-boiled eggs, snails, shellfish and baby squid served warm and together on a large platter. The selection should always reflect the best of what the season offers.

Having established that the *aïoli* is the real star of this recipe, I have spared you the laborious salt cod soaking process, replacing it with a mere light steaming. For the real McCoy, you are required to soak the cod for 24 hours in the fridge, changing the water every 2–3 hours, and then steam it just before serving. An even more unnecessarily extreme instruction than overnight bean-soaking, which I don't do either, this demands a level of sleep-depriving devotion I could manage only if faced with, say, a child's concussion. It is a perfect illustration of the fundamental differences between French and British attitudes to eating pleasurably. And if it's where you or I draw the line, in Provence no one bats an eyelid. There are mountains of salt cured cod on sale in every market. It is a given that the translucent, delicately salted result is well worth a late night sloshing around in a bunged-up fridge.

FOR 6

About 5 vegetables of various colours, such as potatoes, carrots, beetroot, fennel, leeks, asparagus, green beans, cauliflower, broccoli, artichokes, courgettes, turnip…

1.2–1.5 kg cod fillet

6 hard-boiled eggs

500 g of any combination of cooked winkles, mussels, snails, prawns at a pinch (don't worry if you can't find snails. And don't be tempted to buy shellfish ready-cooked and vacuum-packed, unless your fishmonger has just done it for you, frozen or from a tin; if you can't bear cooking them from scratch, leave them out and simply go with the cod and vegetables)

Salt and freshly ground black pepper

FOR THE AIOLI

4 garlic cloves

A good pinch of fleur de sel (sea salt) – you want a bit of abrasiveness to grind down the garlic

Freshly ground black pepper

2 egg yolks

500 ml olive oil

A little lemon juice

Without wishing to sound undermining, start with the *aïoli* as you may need a couple of attempts. As with ordinary mayonnaise, having the eggs, garlic and oil all at room temperature will help immensely. Make the *aïoli* with a pestle and mortar, or find something pestle-shaped for the crush and grind. A fork won't work. I guess a smooth pebble would. I once used the end of the handle of my rolling pin.

Discard the green centre of the garlic cloves and crush the garlic with the salt and pepper into a smooth paste. Then add the egg yolks, stirring and working them gently into the paste to form an emulsion. Whisk in the olive oil little by little, not too much at a time or the aïoli will separate.

When all the oil is incorporated, add a little lemon juice (even if the purists don't).

Steam or boil all the vegetables separately and keep them warm.

Season the cod well with salt and pepper and steam it until it is just cooked. It should be still slightly pearly in the centre.

Arrange the warm vegetables with the warm cod, eggs and shellfish and/or snails on a large flat platter and serve with crusty bread and the *aïoli*.

Petits pois à la Française

This is a really simple dish. Frozen peas will be fine if you are not using fresh. Serve it with chicken, guinea fowl, veal or any other white meat.

FOR 4

**2 kg fresh peas in their pods,
    or 1 kg frozen peas**

2 carrots

1 lettuce heart

10 – 12 baby or pickling onions

25 g butter

150 g *poitrine fumée* or lardons, cubed

1 teaspoon sugar

Salt and freshly ground black pepper

Prepare the vegetables: shell the peas, slice the carrots finely, cut the lettuce into long slices and peel the onions.

In a heavy-based saucepan, heat the butter and fry the pieces of *poitrine*.

Add the vegetables and the sugar and stir. Put in enough water to cover, bring to a gentle simmer, cover the pan and cook for about 20 minutes.

Season with salt and pepper and serve.

Ratatouille

There are two schools of ratatouille-making. One insists on a labour-intensive system of cooking the vegetables separately and uniting them with some form of tomato sauce at the end for a quick finish. The other has a simpler but longer method in which all the ingredients are stewed very slowly together in the same pan from the start. I think the most important rule to follow is to make this dish in season, when the tomatoes are pungently juicy and, like the other team members, hold maximum flavour. If you aren't happy with the fresh tomatoes, use tinned.

FOR 4–6

3 onions, cut into 2 cm pieces

5 garlic cloves, crushed

2 aubergines, cut into 2cm cubes

3 courgettes, cut into 2cm cubes

4 peppers (2 red, 2 green) deseeded
   and cut into 2cm cubes

4–5 large, ripe and juicy tomatoes,
   skins removed, or a large
   tin of passata (600–750g)

6–8 tablespoons olive oil

1 fresh bay leaf, and sprig each of
   thyme and rosemary

A handful of basil leaves

Salt and freshly ground black pepper

Cook all the vegetables separately, except for the onions and garlic which can go in together, in a little olive oil for 15–20 minutes. Do this either consecutively or simultaneously. The peppers will take a little longer than the aubergines and the courgettes. The tomatoes should bubble a little for only a minute or two, as they will provide the unifying sauce and their moisture shouldn't evaporate completely.

Tip all the ingredients into a large pan. Add the bay leaf, thyme and rosemary. Simmer gently for 30 minutes or so, stirring from time to time. Add a little water and/or olive oil if the ratatouille gets too dry.

Alternatively, heat the olive oil in a deep, large pan, throw in all the ingredients and let them simmer gently, covered, for 1 hour –1 hour 30 minutes.

Season the ratatouille with salt and pepper and the fresh basil torn into pieces. Serve warm or cold, as a starter or accompaniment to grilled meat or fish.

Crudités

Many French family evening meals begin with some kind of raw vegetable – not so much a first course but as a reflex akin to serving bread. My children eat them as a starter at their school lunches, and they are expected to then eat more vegetables with their main course. It's a healthy habit to get into and a good way of reconnecting taste buds to pure raw flavour. This is easily done in France, of course, where weekly local markets mean the produce is never far from the place or the moment it was harvested.

FOR 4

FOR THE VINAIGRETTE

1 teaspoon Dijon mustard

1 tablespoon white wine vinegar

4 tablespoons olive oil

Salt and freshly ground black pepper

2 tomatoes, thinly sliced

¹/₂ lettuce

1 cucumber, cut into chunks

2–4 tablespoons crème fraîche or single cream

2 large carrots, grated

Juice of 1 orange, or some vinaigrette

To make the vinaigrette, mix the mustard and vinegar into a smooth paste. Mix in the oil little by little and season with salt and pepper.

Arrange the tomatoes on a quarter of a plate and drizzle a little vinaigrette on them.

Toss the lettuce with the remaining vinaigrette and place on another quarter of the plate.

Mix the cucumber with the cream and place on the third quarter of the plate.

In a separate bowl, mix the carrots with the orange juice or a little vinaigrette and serve on the remaining quarter of the plate.

Carottes Vichy

The naturally effervescent mineral water from the springs at Vichy, reputed to have medicinal benefits, was traditionally used to poach the carrots, thus imparting its distinctive taste. It is now argued that bicarbonate of soda, usually found in sparkling water, is not the best substance for maintaining the carrots' vitamin levels but if you can find 'eau de vichy' (the label St Yorre qualifies) you will at least have full marks for historical precision. If not, read Jeffrey Steingarten's *The Man Who Ate Everything*, a hilarious account of how he found the perfect water. Use the most characterful mineral water you can find and add a little salt.

Today our French home cook would rarely use a whole bottle of mineral water to boil carrots, but will not scrimp on the sugar and butter for that perfect shiny glaze, or the fresh parsley as garnish and flavour enhancer.

**500g fresh young carrots, cut
 into ¹/₂cm slices**

**1 litre Vichy water such as St Yorre,
 or any mineral water**

2 teaspoons sugar

50g butter

1 tablespoon chopped curly parsley

**Add a pinch of salt if not using
 eau de Vichy**

Put the carrots and the water into a saucepan, bring to the boil and simmer, uncovered, until the carrots are tender and most of the water has evaporated. (Drain off the excess rather than have too much liquid. The carrots must sit in the liquid, not swim in it). Add the sugar and butter and glaze the carrots as the butter and sugar melt.

Serve immediately, sprinkled with parsley.

Endives braisées   Braised endives

Also known as *chicons*, or *chicorée*, endives are a popular vegetable in the north of France and Belgium. Bitterness is their main characteristic and they always need to strike up some sort of culinary partnership, be they cooked or raw. Combined with Granny Smith apples, hazelnuts and blue cheese they make a very quick and refreshingly crunchy salad. Boiled for 30 minutes or so, wrapped in ham, topped with a béchamel sauce (see page 120) and given a quick blast under the grill, they become a hearty evening meal. Their tightly packed leaves have the advantage over looser salads of staying fresh and crisp for several days in the fridge.

This is a simple light way of preparing them, with lemon juice to add a touch of acidity and honey to counteract the bitterness. It makes a good accompaniment to any roast meat, especially duck, beef or ham.

4–6 endives

50g butter

Juice of 1 lemon

**1 tablespoon honey, or sugar if
 you prefer**

Salt and freshly ground black pepper

Remove the hard, very bitter base of the endives, and peel away any browned or damaged leaves.

In a wide, shallow saucepan with a lid, melt the butter until it starts to brown.

Turn the endives in the butter for a few minutes until they are golden all over, then add the lemon juice, honey or sugar and enough water to just cover them. (Instead of water, for extra flavour you could use a stock matching whichever meat you are serving.)

Bring to the boil, half cover and simmer gently for around 30 minutes or until they are tender at their base.

Drain off excess water or stock, season and serve.

Tarte au citron

If every French home cook doesn't bake every tart in the book (let alone this book) there will almost certainly be one she makes particularly well. As with quiche, good-quality ready-made pastry is perfectly acceptable to a pastry expert when the filling is good.

Professionals, of course, pride themselves on the perfect base/filling match. The most fabulous *tarte au citron* in Paris can be taken away from Alain Ducasse's little-known deli or *boulang'épicerie* on Avenue de Courcelles. It is an individual version with a wafer-thin pastry case filled with passion-fruit-flavoured citrus filling, smoother than crème brûlée and tarter than lemon curd.

Here are two recipes: one in which the lemon filling is baked with the pastry from the word go; and another in which the pastry case is baked blind for a while, keeping the filling creamier.

FOR 8

FOR THE PASTRY

130g plain flour

70g sugar

1 egg yolk

60g cold salted butter, diced

FOR THE LEMON FILLING

3 egg yolks

50g sugar

Zest and juice of 3 lemons

75g butter

Sift the flour into a mixing bowl and mix in the sugar. Add the egg yolk, then little by little with your fingers, the diced butter.

With your fingers, rub the butter, flour and sugar until the mixture resembles breadcrumbs. Press this crumbly mixture into a 22cm tart dish with your fingers, and put it in the fridge to chill for about 2 hours.

Preheat the oven to 180°C/350°F/gas mark 4.

To make the lemon filling, put the egg yolks and the sugar in a saucepan and beat with a whisk or with electric beaters until the mixture whitens. Add the lemon zest and juice.

Put the saucepan on a low heat and stir gently. Add the butter a little at a time, continuing to stir. When the mixture has thickened, pour it into the chilled tart base and bake in the oven for about 20 minutes, until the filling forms a golden crust.

Serve the tart cold or still slightly warm.

FOR 8

FOR THE PASTRY

175g flour
100g cold salted butter, diced
1 tablespoon sugar
(alternatively, use ready-made
  pâte sablée)

FOR THE LEMON FILLING

5 medium eggs
125g sugar
4 lemons
100g unsalted butter, melted

Sift the flour into a mixing bowl and add the diced butter. With the tips of your fingers, rub the butter into the flour until the mixture resembles fine breadcrumbs. Mix in the sugar.

Make a well in the centre and pour in 2 tablespoons very cold water. Work the mixture into a firm dough with your hands, forming a ball.

On a cold, floured surface (marble is ideal), roll out the pastry thinly enough to fit a 22cm tart dish. Lift it in with the rolling pin and trim the edges. Cover it with foil and chill in the fridge for about 45 minutes.

Preheat the oven to 180°C/350°F/gas mark 4.

Weigh the foiled pastry shell down with some dried beans and bake it for 12–15 minutes.

While the base is in the oven, make the lemon filling. Whisk the eggs and the sugar lightly. Mix in the zest from two of the lemons and the juice from all four, and then the melted butter.

Remove the foil from the pastry base, pour the lemon mixture into it and return it to the oven for a further 20 minutes or so, until the filling is set and the pastry golden.

Remove the tart from the oven and let it cool before serving.

Tarte tatin

The Tatin sisters' fortunate lack of concentration and its resulting 'upside-down' masterpiece is a 19th-century tale well known to foodies. I find the story interesting mainly because they owned up and rejoiced in accidental discovery. Among recipes of mine that I can really call original, many have grown from disasters or near disasters. Diving in, making mistakes then making the best of them is the most effective way of learning. After all, it's only food.

My version is extremely simple. You cannot go wrong – so no chance of making an all-new classic from a catastrophe here. It is a wonderful recipe to have in your repertoire. It looks impressive, is always a hit with guests and kindly allows itself to be prepped to a maximum fuss-free degree. If you possess a cast-iron frying pan, or those cute little blini pans, you can even cook the tarte from start to finish in one piece of equipment.

FOR 6

3 or 4 good tart apples
100 g caster sugar, plus
    2–3 tablespoons
75 g salted butter
1 sheet ready-rolled puff pastry
A dash of Calvados or Pommeau
    (apple brandy)
200 ml crème fraîche

If you are cooking the tarte in one go, preheat the oven to 180°C/350°F/gas mark 4.

Peel, core and quarter the apples.

In a cast-iron frying pan or any heavy-based pan, heat the 100 g of sugar with 2 tablespoons water. When a syrup has formed, let it bubble gently until it begins to caramelise. Swirl the pan about to help spread the caramelisation throughout the syrup (do not stir with a spoon or it will crystallise). When it has reached a golden brown colour (1–2 minutes), take the pan off the heat and add the butter. The caramel will splutter and spit. Stir it very gently with a wooden spoon until it becomes smooth.

Add the quartered apples and cook them gently for 3–4 minutes in the hot caramel. Pop the pan back on a low heat if the caramel has solidified. Taking care not to burn your fingers, arrange the apple quarters in a spiral or concentric circles. If you will be cooking the tarte in a cake tin, arrange the apples in it and pour the caramel from the pan over them.

If you are preparing the tarte for cooking later, let the apples cool down before putting the pastry on top. Leave the tarte in a cool place (the fridge is too cold) until you are ready to cook it.

If cooking the tarte in one go, place the puff pastry on the apples and tuck it around them like a blanket on a bed. Put the pan or tin in the oven and cook for about 25 minutes, until the pastry is golden.

Take the tarte out of the oven and let it stand for about 5 minutes before turning it out onto a deep plate to catch all the caramel and cooking juices.

Mix the 2–3 tablespoons sugar with the Calvados or Pommeau, stir in the cream and serve with the hot tarte. It will also be delicious with plain crème fraîche, double or clotted cream or vanilla ice cream.

Soufflé au fromage   Cheese soufflé

Many of my French contemporaries grew up on cheese soufflé or vegetable soup for dinner. Soufflé is one of those mythically difficult, potentially humiliating dishes. The cheese version is easiest as it melts into the batter to allow an easy rise, as long as you refrain from opening the oven door to take a peek while it's cooking. But then everybody knows that.

FOR 4

35 g butter

50 g plain flour

250 ml full-fat milk

2 egg yolks, plus 5 egg whites

**75 g grated gruyère, cantal or
   beaufort cheese**

Pinch of ground nutmeg

Salt and freshly ground black pepper

FOR GREASING THE SOUFFLÉ DISH

15 g butter

1 level tablespoon flour

Preheat the oven to 200°C/400°F/gas mark 6.

Grease and flour a 14 cm diameter, 8 cm high soufflé dish, then leave it in the fridge.

Melt the butter for the soufflé in a saucepan, add the flour and cook for a few minutes, stirring continuously with a whisk or a wooden spoon. When the roux is a golden colour, add the milk little by little, again stirring as you go.

Bring to the boil and remove from the heat. Let the béchamel sauce cool for a few minutes before beating in the egg yolks, then the cheese. Season with the nutmeg, some pepper and some salt.

Whisk the egg whites until they are moderately stiff, like whipped Italian ice cream.

Add a little beaten egg white to the cheese mixture with a large metal spoon, to loosen it up. Then gently fold in the remaining egg white.

Spoon the soufflé batter gently into the mould and cook for 20–25 minutes if you can see into your oven. Take a look at 23 minutes if not. Remove from the oven and serve immediately.

Crêpes Suzette

In France, crêperies have withstood the pizza/sushi onslaught and are as popular as ever. There are five in my town alone. A brand-new, Breton-blue one opened just a month ago. They are the perfect family restaurant, holding no surprises, economical, usually with pretty quick service and an infinite choice of combinations, sweet or savoury, to please the pickiest six-year-old.

Making crêpes at home is another matter, however, for it is very difficult to cook them fast enough to satisfy everyone's appetite. I once had a fabulous nanny who was an ace at making them and often I would come home to the enormous, neat pile she had whipped up in a spare half hour at some point during the day. They reheat very well in the microwave and where eggs and cheese were requested, it was a cinch to pop four back into the pan.

For a more sophisticated dessert, here is the traditional recipe that elevates the humble crêpe to Suzette status. If you see them on the menu in a typical brasserie, the chances are they will be cooked at the table before you. Never miss the opportunity to see the show and pick up a bit of technique.

MAKES ABOUT 12 CRÊPES DEPENDING ON SIZE OF PAN

FOR THE CRÊPE BATTER

125 g plain flour

3 eggs

2 tablespoons sunflower oil

75 g salted butter, melted

3 tablespoons sugar

350 ml full-fat milk

FOR THE ORANGE SAUCE

100 g salted butter

100 g sugar

8 tablespoons Grand Marnier or Cointreau liqueur

3 tablespoons brandy

Zest and juice of 1 orange

50 g butter, for the cooking

Sift the flour into a bowl and make a well in the centre. Add all the other batter ingredients and stir well with a whisk, working out any lumps that form. Let the batter rest in the fridge for a good hour.

To make the sauce, put the butter in a small saucepan, add the sugar, 2 tablespoons Grand Marnier or Cointreau and 1 tablespoon brandy, and the orange zest and juice. Bring to the boil, stirring continuously, then cook briskly until the sauce thickens.

To cook the crêpes, heat a little of the 50 g of butter in a crêpe pan. Ladle a little batter into the centre, tilting the pan so that the batter covers the surface thinly and evenly. Cook for about 20 seconds, then flip the crêpe over and cook for a further 20 seconds until it is golden brown. Slide it out of the pan onto a warmed plate and keep warm as you make the rest, melting a little butter in the pan for each one.

To serve, pour the sauce into a frying pan over a low heat. Put the crêpes in the sauce one at a time, folding them once, and then again, to make little triangles. Spoon the sauce over the crêpes to make sure they are all soaked with sauce.

Warm the remaining Grand Marnier and brandy in a small saucepan. At the table, pour it over the crêpes in the pan, ignite for a magnificent flambé and serve.

Iles flottantes   Floating islands

Our *Française* knows that, having mastered the daunting *crème anglaise* (custard), the world is her sauceboat. Chocolate sauce, coffee sauce, praline sauce, vanilla ice cream, *crème pâtissière* and *crème au beurre* are all derivatives and variations. Floating islands, also known as *oeufs à la neige* (snowy eggs), is an impressive, billowing dessert that happily uses up the egg whites left over from the custard-making process. I always make my 'islands' in the microwave; indeed, the results are so good I reckon that must be why the machine was invented.

FOR 8

1 litre full-fat milk
1 vanilla pod, split lengthways
8 eggs, separated
250 g sugar, plus 100 g for the caramel

Bring the milk to the boil with the vanilla pod. While it is heating, beat the egg yolks with the 250 g of sugar in a large bowl until doubled in volume and pale.

Just before it boils, take the milk off the heat and pour onto the yolks and sugar, stirring with a wooden spoon to mix well.

Pour the mixture back into the saucepan and heat on a medium heat, stirring continuously. Whatever you do, do not let the custard boil. Once you see bubbles bursting on the surface, it is already too late. The trick is to remove the custard from the heat, before it is appropriately thick, as it will continue to thicken in its residual heat – remove the custard from the heat when the mark left by a finger drawn down the back of a custard-coated spoon stays put.

As soon as you feel the custard is ready, pour it out of the hot saucepan into a cold recipient, and continue stirring it. If little lumps have formed, give it a good whisk. When the custard has cooled down, scrape out the vanilla seeds from the pod into the custard and discard the pod.

While the custard is cooling, beat the egg whites until they are very stiff. Directly on the microwave plate (give it a wash beforehand!) spoon out 3–4 eggy 'islands' and, on high, cook them for about 10 seconds; you will know they are ready when you see them swell as if they were breathing in very slowly, about to sigh. Slide them off the plate onto a flat dish. Make another batch or two and let them chill in the fridge, along with the custard.

Not too long before serving (about 1 hour maximum, but best just before) make the caramel. In a heavy-based saucepan, heat the sugar with 2 tablespoons water. The sugar will dissolve to form a syrup. Let this bubble away until it begins to caramelise, turning a golden brown. This won't happen uniformly, but whatever you do, do not stir the caramel otherwise it will crystallize. Instead, tilt the saucepan to evenly distribute the golden sugar until it is all a rich mahogany. Don't let it burn.

Pour the custard into a deep serving bowl and float the egg-white 'islands' on top. Dip a teaspoon into the caramel, then, holding the spoon high above the serving bowl, let strands of caramel fall onto the islands. Zigzag across them to create a web-like effect.

Leave the dish in a cool place (note that the caramel might liquefy if the dish is put in the fridge) until ready to serve.

Crème brûlée

This has been an immensely popular dish for the past ten years. It is another the French like to think of as theirs, when in fact it originated in the sixteenth century in the UK as burnt cream and in Spain in the eighteenth as 'crema catalana'. The crème brulée's eggy neutrality and textural uniformity has been used as a base for all sorts of imaginative variations, sweet and savoury. One of the most famous, a contemporary foie gras version on a bed of cranberries, pears and walnuts, is well and truly French and thought up by the great pâtissier, Pierre Hermé.

In this, the classic recipe, it is important to caramelise the sugar quickly, so that the cold custard underneath doesn't warm up, or indeed, cook further. A little blowtorch is perfect; if you have to use your grill, make sure it is red hot before putting the crème dishes as close to it as you can.

FOR 6

800 ml single cream

2 vanilla pods, split lengthways

6 egg yolks

150 g white sugar

80 g coarse brown sugar

Bring the cream to the boil with the vanilla pods, then remove it from the heat and leave to infuse for 15–20 minutes.

Preheat the oven to 110°C/225°F/gas mark $1/4$.

With a wooden spoon, gently mix the egg yolks with the sugar.

Scrape the vanilla seeds into the cream and discard the pods. Add the cream to the egg mixture and mix well.

Pour the mixture into 6 individual shallow ramekins and bake for 1 hour until just set. Remove them from the oven and leave to cool, then chill them in the fridge for 5–6 hours.

Just before serving, sprinkle the tops with the brown sugar and caramelise with a blowtorch or under a very hot grill.

Clafouti aux cerises   Baked cherry custard

Clafoutis is a sort of fluffy crêpe batter cooked with fruit, and as with so many other dishes, opinions differ about how it should be cooked. With this dessert everyone argues about whether you should stone the cherries and spare your teeth, or leave them whole for better taste, less work and a lot of more or less discreet stone-spitting into palms. Lazy as I am, I much prefer the stones in. This is a fantastic store-cupboard staple, as preserved cherries are juicier, and often better tasting, than average-quality fresh ones.

FOR 8

20g butter

5 eggs

150g sugar, plus extra for sprinkling

15g (1 sachet) vanilla sugar, or a few
   drops of vanilla extract

80g plain flour

500ml full-fat milk

1kg cherries

Preheat the oven to 190°C/375°F/gas mark 5.

Use the butter to grease a medium-sized ovenproof gratin dish.

Beat the eggs with the sugar and vanilla sugar. Add the flour and then the milk and extract, if using, mixing well to avoid lumps.

Put the cherries in the dish and pour the batter over them. Bake the clafoutis for around 45 minutes until golden. Remove from the oven and leave to cool before sprinkling it with sugar and serving. It is also very good completely cold.

Baba au rhum   Rum baba

This is a very quick version, unfettered by yeast or yeast-induced resting times.

FOR 6–8

3 medium eggs, separated
125 g caster sugar
50 g unsalted butter, melted
1/2 teaspoon vanilla extract
Zest of 1 lemon
4 tablespoons warm full-fat milk
150 g plain flour
2 teaspoons baking powder

FOR THE SYRUP
150 g sugar
150 ml brown rum

100 ml whipping cream, whipped,
for serving

Preheat the oven to 180°C/350°F/gas mark 4.

Grease and lightly flour a savarin mould.

Beat the egg yolks with the sugar until the mixture becomes pale and creamy. Add the melted butter, vanilla extract, lemon zest, warm milk, flour and baking powder and mix well.

Whisk the egg whites until stiff peaks form and fold them gently into the mixture. Pour it into the prepared mould and cook for 20–25 minutes until golden on top and firm to touch.

Remove the baba from the oven and leave it to cool before turning it out of the mould.

To make the syrup, heat 500 ml water with the sugar until the sugar has dissolved. Let the syrup cool completely before adding the rum.

Pour the rum syrup over the baba and set aside until the syrup is completely absorbed. Serve with whipped cream.

Every French home cook does a great chocolate cake. Very often served simply with some good-quality vanilla ice cream, it's always a hit. This one is dangerously rich, more of a cooked mousse than a cake, with a tablespoon of flour added as an afterthought.

Tarte au chocolat Chocolate tart

This is my favourite chocolate tart recipe, given to me by another fanatical chocolate lover and adapted from a fantastic Joël Robuchon creation in the late 1990s, when very bitter chocolate was becoming very fashionable. The tricky bit my friend left out was 'beurre pommade', very soft butter that was meant to be incorporated into the chocolate cream at a certain temperature before baking. It is an amazingly rich tart, even without the extra butter.

FOR 8

FOR THE PASTRY

70g icing sugar

80g unsalted butter, softened

3 egg yolks

180g plain flour, sifted

FOR THE CHOCOLATE CREAM FILLING

200ml single cream

200g good-quality dark chocolate, minimum 60% cocoa solids

1 egg, beaten

80ml full-fat milk

To make the pastry, mix the icing sugar into the butter. Add the egg yolks and mix a little more. Drop in the flour in one go and stir it in quickly.

Roll the pastry into a ball, cover it with clingfilm and chill in the fridge for about 1 hour.

Roll out the pastry and press it into a 20cm tart dish. Put in the fridge for 30 minutes. Preheat the oven to 200°C/400°F/gas mark 6.

Bake the tart base for about 10 minutes. Remove it from the oven and reduce the oven temperature to 150°C/300°F/gas mark 2.

To make the chocolate cream filling, bring the cream to the boil and then remove from the heat. Break the chocolate into small pieces and melt it in the cream. Let the chocolate cream cool for about 10 minutes.

Mix in the beaten egg and the milk, then pour the cream into the tart base. Return it to the cooler oven for 15–18 minutes – the filling should be just set, still a bit wobbly when you tap the side of the dish.

Leave the tart to cool slightly, and serve just warm with some double cream.

Fondant au chocolat Melt-in-your-mouth chocolate cake

FOR 8 (photographed opposite)

200g good-quality dark chocolate, minimum 65% cocoa solids

1 tablespoon double-strength espresso coffee, hot

200g butter, softened

200g sugar

5 eggs

1 heaped tablespoon plain flour

Preheat the oven to 180°C/350°F/gas mark 4. Grease and flour a 25cm sandwich tin.

Break the chocolate into small pieces and put them in a mixing bowl, then set the bowl over a saucepan of barely simmering water. Pour the hot coffee onto the chocolate and stir until the chocolate has melted. Add the butter and let it melt into the chocolate.

Add the sugar and stir well, then break the eggs into the mixture one at a time, stirring well after each addition. Finally mix in the flour.

Pour the mixture into the sandwich tin and bake for 20–25 minutes. The cake should be still very moist in the centre.

Remove from the oven and leave to cool completely before turning out. Wrap the cake in foil and try to resist eating it for at least a day. It will taste so much better.

new classics

This section is a peek at what a food-fashion-conscious *maîtresse de maison* is serving today. It is also an illustration of how French cooks master a cooking technique and then change around the ingredients to create something at once new but familiar. It's not just a question of substituting apples for pears... sweet becomes savoury, fish becomes meat, fruit becomes vegetable, not one flavour is used but three in smaller portions...

These new classics have also helped change the very structure of a typical French dinner party. With more slow-cooked, one-pot dishes such as tagine or bourguignon being produced, guests simply don't have room for starters AND cheese. Very often the aperitif becomes more consequential, with a tapas-style mini dish or two being served with drinks.

Over the past five years or so the French have been looking more and more outside the 'hexagon', of the coutry's borders for inspiration. Food from Tunisia, Morocco, Réunion Island and the French West Indies is no longer confined to specialist restaurants and caterers. With the more ready availability of foreign spices and ingredients, and a heightened curiosity about exotic food, many dishes from ex-colonies are now being cooked at home.

In my local supermarket, Monday night is couscous night. A huge cooking stand is set up, with three-metre-wide cauldrons containing the couscous grains, harissa-poached vegetables and an assortment of meat to take away. In Marrakech and Essouaria, residential cooking courses are becoming more and more popular. It's a deliciously peaceful and relaxing way to spend a long weekend, hidden away in a riad deep in the Médina. The celebrity chef and food historian, Fatema Hal, has her own slot on the French cooking cable channel and a very chic collection of spices and rubs sold in the most select of Paris's *épiceries fines*.

The *bistronamanie* (bistro cooking) craze of recent years has brought once old-fashioned, comforting classics such as *pot au feu*, *hachis*, and *tarte tatins* back onto chic tables. In the Eighties, serving *blanquette* or *poule au pot* at home was considered deeply uncool. This was food linked to days when women felt they were chained to their stoves. Thanks to chefs Yves Camdeborde and Alain Ducasse, these traditional, reassuring recipes, right at the heart of France's culinary identity, became popular again.

Foreign dishes are also thus remixed *à la Française* and curries, ceviches and tiramisus have become fiercely trendy. The UK, Italy and Spain are sources of new classics that the French have made their own. Now crumbles, cakes and muffins are often on teatime menus. Risotto and carpaccios, sweet and savoury, are favourite dinner party standards and the tapas craze has made mini-tasting portions hot as appetisers.

Soup was once considered extremely dull but now both sweet and savoury versions are very popular. The new interest in neglected root vegetables sees many of them transformed into creamy veloutés as a start to many meals.

More amusingly cakes, crumbles and trifles are now common in both sweet and savoury versions. Their popularity grew thanks to their slightly subversive appeal, but in France, *la cuisine anglaise* is still considered a bit of a joke. It would appear that most French people who experienced British home cooking did so on a horrendous cultural or linguistic exchange somewhere near Bolton. Horror stories are still recounted with an appalled drama, no matter how many Michelin stars are awarded to London restaurants.

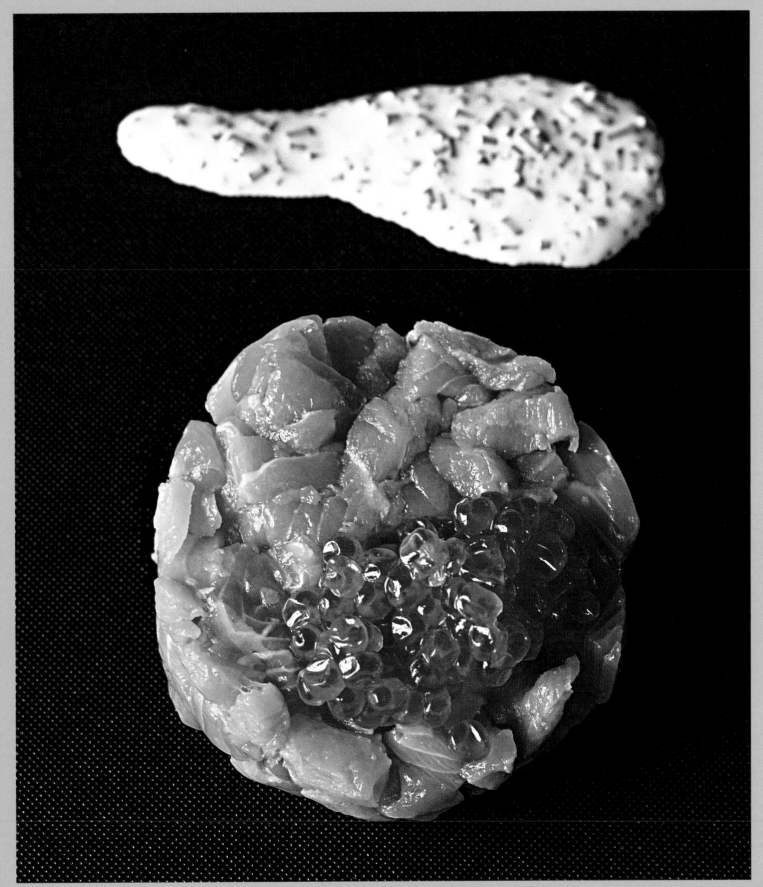

Tartare de saumon

Two-salmon tartare with pink peppercorns and a light herb cream

The popularity of raw fish is growing rapidly in France. The onslaught of sushi and curiosity about ceviches (although it's still light on the chilli please) are helping it along. Scallops, tuna, langoustines and salmon are the favourite no-cook options. Every good fishmonger will offer a melting slab of Turkish-delight-red tuna, two to three varieties and cuts of fresh salmon (Label Rouge Scottish is still considered to be top of the range) and scallops in the shell or pre-prepared and ready to cook.

Here, raw and smoked salmon take the place of challenging raw beef, and the creamy sauce smooths everything along in an altogether more genteel way than the raw egg yolks of the original meaty version. It's an example of a successful gastronomical travesty. If you can't find *baies roses* (pink pepper), use a mild or suitably flavoured pepper (with lemon, fennel or coriander), coarsely ground for the crunch. Do make the effort to form the little tartares in ramekins, or even easier, a pastry cutter. If you are going freestyle, nothing short of a perfectly formed quenelle will do.

FOR 4 (photographed on page 153)

400 g of the best, freshest raw salmon steaks or fillet you can find

4 medium slices of good-quality smoked salmon

2 tablespoons *baies roses* (pink peppercorns, optional

Fleur de sel (sea salt)

1–2 tablespoons light olive oil

2–3 tablespoons finely chopped fresh herbs such as chives, dill, basil and sorrel

1 small shallot or spring onion, very finely chopped

150 ml single cream

Salt and freshly ground black pepper

Salmon roe, to garnish

1 lemon or lime, for serving

Make sure both types of salmon are well chilled. If you are using fresh salmon steaks, remove the skin. Cut the fresh salmon into small cubes. Cut the smoked salmon into small pieces compatible *en bouche* with their raw brothers. Mix the two salmons with the *baies roses*, if using, some *fleur de sel* and olive oil.

Mix the herbs and the shallot or spring onion with the cream. Season with salt and pepper.

In a small ramekin or with a pastry cutter, form little circles of salmon and place them on four individual plates. Pour the cream around the tartares, drop some salmon roe on top and squeeze some lemon or lime juice over. Serve immediately.

Canard à la vanille

Vanilla duck

The Island of Réunion is famous for its vanilla crops. This is one of their most celebrated dishes and a great way of getting some life out of dried and dusty vanilla pods.

FOR 4–5

1 duck, cut into pieces
2 onions, chopped
1 carrot, chopped
4 tomatoes, quartered
2–3 vanilla pods, split lengthways
1 bay leaf
Salt and freshly ground black pepper

Heat a large, heavy-bottomed casserole dish and brown the duck all over. You won't need any fat as the duck skin will release its fat as you begin to cook it. Remove the duck pieces and discard any burned or excess fat.

Add the onions and carrot to the casserole dish and cook for a few minutes, stirring frequently. Add the tomatoes, then the duck pieces, vanilla pods and bay leaf. Stir well, then add enough water to reach about halfway up the duck. Bring to the boil and simmer for about 40–45 minutes, until the meat is tender and coming away from the bone. Add more water if you feel it is all drying out too quickly.

Season to taste and serve with rice.

Risotto de petit épeautre à la truffe

Spelt risotto with truffles

Spelt (*épeautre*) is a subspecies of common wheat, surviving as a relic crop in Italy and central Europe. As the health-food market takes hold in France, spelt's nutty taste is more and more appreciated in soups and salads. It behaves much like rice when cooked in a risotto-ish way, only with a little added crunch.

FOR 4

¹/₂ leek, cut into chunks

1 carrot, cut into chunks

1 onion, quartered

¹/₂ golden turnip, cut into chunks

750 ml chicken stock

200 g spelt

1 bouquet garni

150 g butter

1 fresh black truffle, about 20 g, sliced or grated

Salt and freshly ground black pepper

Steam or boil the vegetables, leaving them slightly firm, and set aside.

Bring the chicken stock to the boil, add the spelt and the bouquet garni, and cook for about 45 minutes, stirring frequently, until the spelt has absorbed the stock.

Melt a third of the butter in a frying pan, add the vegetables and cook briefly, stirring, to warm through the glaze.

Stir the remaining butter through the spelt, mix in the vegetables, season if necessary, scatter the truffle on top and serve.

Taboulé

Rumour has it that this Lebanese-labelled salad originated somewhere between Turkey, Iraq and Syria, and that pomegranate juice was first used instead of lemon in its sauce. The poorer and more arid the country, the more it was considered a luxury to include lots of fresh herbs. The herb and bulgur wheat proportions vary a lot in France, where *taboulé* is a popular accompaniment to barbecues or 'méchoui' (spit-roasted meat).

FOR 6

150 g bulgur wheat

4 good-sized bunches of flat-leaf parsley (like those in the photo), very finely chopped

3 good-sized bunches of mint, very finely chopped

8 tomatoes, skinned and deseeded

6 shallots, very finely chopped

Juice of 6 medium lemons

10–12 tablespoons extra virgin olive oil

Prepare the bulgur wheat according to the instructions on the packet or sachet.

Mix the parsley and mint with the tomatoes, shallots and bulgur.

Pour on the lemon juice and the olive oil, season with salt and pepper, mix lightly and let the salad rest and chill in the fridge for a good 2 hours before serving.

Ragoût de Cabri   Corsican goat stew

The food of Corsica is hearty and robust. The flavours and produce of the *maquis*, the mountain scrub, are as present as those of the sea. Goat meat or 'cabri' is commonly used in many dishes. Use pork or chicken if you are not in Corsica.

FOR 4–6

3 tablespoons olive oil

1kg potatoes, chopped into chunks

1.5–2 kg goat meat, cut into
bite-sized chunks

3 onions, chopped finely

3 garlic cloves, crushed

2 bay leaves

Sprigs of thyme, sage and rosemary

A small handful of flat-leaf parsley,
chopped

2 tablespoons plain flour

3–4 tablespoons tomato purée or
passata or chopped tinned tomatoes

250 ml full-bodied red wine, Corsican
if you can find it

Salt and freshly ground black pepper

Heat the oil in a large, heavy-based saucepan and fry the potatoes for a few minutes to brown them. Remove from the pan and set aside.

Add the meat to the pan, along with the onions, garlic, herbs and parsley, and sprinkle the flour over the lot. Brown for a few minutes, stirring as you go, then pour in the tomatoes and the wine.

Mix thoroughly, add a little salt and pepper and bring to the boil, then cover the pan, reduce the heat and simmer very gently for about 45 minutes.

Add the potatoes and continue simmering for a further 30 minutes, until the meat is tender.

Adjust the seasoning to taste and serve.

Velouté de potiron   Pumpkin soup

Pumpkin is a tremendously popular vegetable in France. Pumpkin purée mixed with potatoes is a very common alternative to plain mashed potatoes come the autumn.

FOR 4

500 g pumpkin, peeled and cut into
chunks

2 smallish potatoes (about 100 g)
peeled and cut into chunks

1 garlic clove, crushed

150–200ml single cream

A good pinch each of cumin, nutmeg
and cinnamon (all ground)

1 tart apple (Granny Smith)

Salt and freshly ground black pepper

Put the pumpkin, potatoes and garlic into a pan with about 750 ml boiling water. Bring to the boil, cover and simmer for about 30 minutes.

Put the soup into a blender and liquidise. Add the cream (adjust quantity according to taste and thickness) and spices and season with salt and pepper. Add a little water if it is too thick.

Grate the apple into the soup just before serving.

Crumble à la ratatouille   Ratatouille crumble

In perhaps the most unlikely and spectacular British culinary putsch for decades, French sandwich bars and supermarkets shelves now carry ready-made crumbles, crumblesque desserts and even yogurts with crumble toppings.

A far cry from the school-lunch nightmares of my childhood, the French versions, produced by applying the principle of a crunchy topping, gradually softening and soaked into by a poached base, can be fascinating. The worst I ever tried had a dark chocolate base. This one of the best. It could be edible proof of the existence of *l'entente cordiale*, as if we needed it.

FOR 4

4 tablespoons olive oil

1 onion, finely chopped

2 garlic cloves, crushed

1 aubergine, cubed

1 red pepper, cut into strips

1 green pepper, cut into strips

**3 courgettes, peeled if you like
  and cut into chunks**

1 kg tomatoes, skinned and deseeded

Fresh thyme and rosemary

FOR THE CRUMBLE TOPPING

**100 g very cold salted butter,
  finely diced**

150 g plain flour

80 g parmesan cheese, grated

50 g pine nuts, toasted

Freshly ground black pepper

Heat the olive oil in a frying pan and fry the onion and garlic. Add the aubergine and the red and green peppers. When they have softened, add the courgettes, tomatoes and herbs, some salt and pepper, and cook for a further 10–15 minutes until cooked.

While the vegetables are cooking, preheat the oven to 180°C/350°F/gas mark 4 and prepare *le crumbeul*. In a food-processor, or with your fingers, rub the butter into the flour and parmesan. When you have a mixture resembling breadcrumbs, mix in the toasted pine nuts and some pepper.

Put the cooked vegetables into a gratin dish, cover them with the crumble mixture and cook in the oven for about 30 minutes or until the top is golden and crispy.

Serve hot or warm, with a crisp salad or as an accompaniment to roast lamb, chicken or fish.

Cake aux olives, ail et romarin

Olive, garlic and rosemary cake

The celebrity chef Sophie Dudemaine has sold 1 million copies of her book *Les Cakes de Sophie*, a collection of savoury and sweet cake recipes all using a base batter of eggs, oil or butter, and flour. The convergence of the popularity of English teatime items (fruitcake, scones, muffins and brownies) with the need to get a balanced meal on the table in 26 minutes, the average time spent in a French kitchen of an evening, has made Sophie a household name.

The stodgy, traditional 'cake aux olives' was for a long time relegated to the plastic-coated, E-number depths of hypermarket shelves. Now French home cooks are serving it up with salad on the side as an evening meal. I don't cook it often, as I find the carb/protein ratio a bit heavy for a main course in the evening, but it is great as filling-aperitif-merging-into-salad-as-starters. And once you master the batter, you can mix and match the most unlikely ingredients.

FOR 4–6

120 g lardons
150 g plain flour, sifted
2 teaspoons baking powder
6 medium eggs
50 ml single cream
6 tablespoons olive oil
100 g black olives, sliced
100 g parmesan cheese, grated
Fleur de sel (sea salt) and
   freshly ground black pepper

Preheat the oven to 180°C/350°F/gas mark 4.

Grill or fry the lardons until they are crispy, then leave to cool.

Put the flour and the baking powder into a mixing bowl. With a whisk, beat in the eggs (start with two), then the cream and the olive oil.

Mix in the lardons, olives and cheese, and season with pepper and a little salt. Pour into a 20 cm cake tin and bake for 35 minutes.

Turn the cake out and let it cool slightly before slicing and serving.

Pot au feu de canard aux épices douces

Duck pot au feu with gentle spices

This is a faster-cooking, more delicately flavoured version of the beefy institution that is *pot au feu* (see page 121). As foie gras consumption increases, so the French are eating more duck meat. My children love it. Pan-fried with big black cherries and served with steamed broccoli, it makes a swift and easy weekday meal. *Filets* and *aiguillettes* are from the breast of ducks that have not been reared for foie gras, whereas the more noble *magret* designates meaty breasts from the *canard gras* and are covered with a sumptuous layer of fatty skin. Usually the legs and thighs of a foie gras duck are cooked in duck fat and thus become *confit*, sold preserved in tins or vacuum-packed.

I have given a quick version of this *pot au feu*. The duck legs are poached in chicken stock; you could use ready-made stock, but if you always use home-made chicken stock anyway, why not make everything a little more difficult for yourself, and the dish tastier, by having your butcher remove the breasts and legs of a whole duck and then use its carcass to make delicious duck stock before poaching the meat? You could also add a *cuisse de canard confite* for extra flavour, though it will make the dish a little more fatty, and more than ever you should cool and skim excess fat from it before serving.

FOR 4

4 uncooked duck legs

1 litre chicken stock

4 carrots, chopped

2 small turnips, chopped

1 leek, green tops removed, chopped

1 parsnip, peeled and chopped

150 g celery, chopped

1 small onion, peeled and studded
   with 4–5 cloves

1/2 teaspoon ground nutmeg

1 small cinnamon stick

Salt and freshly ground black pepper

In a large frying pan, brown the duck legs all over. Drain them on some kitchen paper to remove excess fat.

Pour the stock into a very large pan, add the vegetables and bring to the boil. When boiling, add the spices and the duck legs. Simmer for about 45 minutes, skimming off the fat as it rises to the surface.

When the duck is cooked, remove it from the cooking liquid and serve with the vegetables and stock alongside. (You could also remove the vegetables and reduce the stock further to intensify its flavour.)

Tajine d'agneau aux abricots et pruneaux

Lamb tagine with apricots and prunes

Tagine takes its name from the coned-hat clay dish in which it is cooked. Any heavy-based lidded casserole will do, especially as a hefty Moroccan tagine top is often too tall to fit in a normal oven. The meat (lamb or chicken) is browned with onions and spices, then simmered gently (the longer the better) with dried fruits and vegetables added a little while before serving. Honey, toasted almonds and sesame seeds add sweetness and nuttiness to this rich and aromatic classic.

FOR 6

5–6 tablespoons olive oil

1 shoulder of lamb, deboned, cut into chunks

4 onions, roughly chopped

2 teaspoons ground cinnamon

2 teaspoons ground coriander

2 teaspoons ground cumin

1 teaspoon ground ginger

$\frac{1}{2}$ teaspoon saffron strands

20 dried stoned apricots

20 dried stoned prunes

Salt and freshly ground black pepper

OPTIONAL EXTRAS

A couple of handfuls of almonds or sesame seeds, toasted

1–2 tablespoons honey

Fresh coriander and mint

Heat the oil in the casserole dish, add the meat and onions and brown on a brisk heat. Sprinkle on the spices and continue to cook for a few minutes.

Add enough water to almost cover the meat (leaving about a quarter above water level), stir and scrape the bottom of the casserole to deglaze and bring to the boil. Cover the casserole, add a little salt and pepper, reduce the heat and simmer for a least 1 hour 30 minutes, and up to 2 hours 30 minutes, adding water as it cooks down.

(The dish is best left alone after 2 hours cooking and then reheated the next day. You could also give a nod to tradition and cook the browned meat for a couple of hours in an oven preheated to 130–150°C/275–300°F/gas mark 1–2, stirring from time to time.)

About 20 minutes before serving, add the dried fruits and let them heat through.

If you like, sprinkle with nuts and herbs, swirl in the honey and serve.

Nougat glacé au miel

Nougat and honey ice cream

This is an icy version of the cult *confiserie* in which the twang of raspberries cuts beautifully into the honey-sweet frozen meringue. Mix and match the nuts and candied fruits at will, keeping some over for decoration before serving.

FOR 6

50g whole blanched almonds

30g whole hazelnuts or walnuts

30g pine nuts

50g candied fruit, such as cherries, orange and lemon peel, and angelica, plus extra for decoration

3 egg whites

2 tablespoons runny honey, preferably a flavoured one such as lavender, rosemary or thyme

300ml very chilled whipping cream or whippable double cream

FOR THE COULIS

300g fresh or frozen raspberries

75g sugar

Roughly chop the nuts and the candied fruits. Try to vary the size of the pieces, and leave some whole.

Whisk the egg whites until they form soft peaks.

Heat the honey in a saucepan until it caramelises slightly. Pour it hot onto the egg whites then whisk for a further 2 minutes.

Whip the cream until it is stiff, add the nuts and fruit and fold the mixture gently into the beaten egg whites.

Pour the whole lot into a small loaf tin or a silicone mould and freeze for at least 12 hours.

Cook the raspberries with the sugar to a jam-like consistency. Cool completely before serving with the nougat.

Soupe de fraises, fraises des bois, roses et pistaches

Strawberry and rose soup with pistachios

For the French cook, for a long time there seemed to be no middle ground between complicated, faintly pompous consommés and rich vichyssoise and the humble all-in, dinner vegetable velouté. But soups, hot and cold, savoury and sweet, have enjoyed a renaissance over the past few years. Intensely flavoured dainty glassfuls are served in trendy restaurants as *amuse-bouches*, and *bars à soupe* are springing up around Paris, in tune with the trend towards organic, vegetarian and fair-trade cuisine. At home, they are marvellous make-ahead starters or puddings.

Wild strawberries (*fraises des bois*) are a rare commodity, fragile and therefore difficult to pick and transport, and with a very short shelf life. Their bubblegum pungency is wonderful teamed with the sharper common-or-garden strawberry. If you are in France and can't find them, replace them with the *Mara des Bois* variety, which have a flavour somewhere between wild and common and are available from May all through summer, otherwise find the most flavourful.

FOR 4

750g strawberries

3–4 tablespoons sugar, depending on the sweetness of the fruit

150ml dry white wine (sparkling would be nice)

A dash of rosewater

150g wild strawberries

Pistachios, cut into slivers

Edible rose petals

Wash and hull the ordinary strawberries. In a food-processor, whizz 500g of them into a purée. Sweeten with sugar and dilute with the wine and a little water until you are happy with its souplike consistency. Add the rosewater to taste – there should be just a hint.

Slice the remaining ordinary strawberries and mix them into the soup. Chill thoroughly for a few hours.

Hull and wash the wild strawberries or Mara des Bois gently, and sprinkle them over each plate before serving, along with the pistachio slivers and rose petals.

Trifle aux framboises

Raspberry trifle

The funniest thing about the French making trifle is the way they pronounce the word. They rarely manage a full-blown *treifeul*; it usually comes out as *trifleu* and very often when written an extra 'f' will sneak in to justify the outrageous frenchification of one of Britain's national dishes.

This recipe uses *biscuits roses de Reims*. Ironically, and this is unknown to the French, they are the ultimate trifle-making ingredient. Vastly superior to trifle sponges, boudoir biscuits or even the softer *biscuits à la cuillère*, they crumble, absorb fruit juice and liqueur and impart a delicate pinkness to the layers.

FOR 4

400g fresh raspberries (or unbashed frozen ones)

150g sugar

10–12 biscuits roses de Reims, or about 15 boudoir biscuits

A good splash of *crème de framboises* (raspberry liqueur)

350ml whipping cream

4 egg yolks

Cook half the raspberries with 100g of the sugar until they have a jam-like consistency. Leave to cool.

Crush half the biscuits into 4 glasses. Soak them thoroughly with the *crème de framboise*. Cover them with a layer of the cooked raspberry coulis and leave to chill in the fridge for about 1 hour.

Cover the cooked raspberry layer with more crushed biscuits (keep a little biscuit powder for decoration).

Whip the cream with the egg yolks and 50g sugar and add a layer to the trifles. Top with fresh whole raspberries, a little biscuit powder from the packet, and serve.

Tiramisu aux deux figues

Fig tiramisu

In Saint-Germain-en-Laye, Véronique's tiramisu is almost as legendary as her pesto and vegetable lasagne. Her extra layer of figs is a brilliant addition to a great Italian classic, which has slowly migrated off French restaurant menus and into home kitchens.

FOR 6–8

3 eggs, separated

150 g grandulated or caster sugar

250 g mascarpone cheese

2 tablespoons Amaretto or Marsala

2 boxes boudoir biscuits

500 ml cold strong coffee

4 fresh figs, cut into small chunks

4 dried figs, cut into small chunks

2 tablespoons cocoa powder

Put the egg yolks and sugar into a mixing bowl and beat with an electric whisk until the mixture turns white and doubles in volume. Add the mascarpone and the Amaretto and beat again until the cream is smooth.

Whisk the egg whites until they are stiff, then add them gently to the mascarpone 'cream'.

Quickly dip the boudoir biscuits into the coffee and place them in the base of a gratin dish. Cover the biscuits with half the mascarpone cream.

Mix together the fresh and dried figs and set them on the cream.

Soak another lot of biscuits in the coffee, place them over the figs and top with the remaining mascarpone cream.

Leave the tiramisu to rest in the fridge for at least 2 hours, preferably overnight. Before serving, dust the top with cocoa powder.

chapter 3

steals from chefs

The French debate everything with verve, passion and unrelenting self-righteousness: from who should leave an overloaded lift, or who should leave the national football team, to who should leave the Elysée Palace (the official residence of the President). Food, cooking and the restaurant business are discussed passionately, as matters of national concern. People who never have and never will dine in starred chefs' restaurants constantly argue about what they will never eat there.

If you feel like livening things up at the bar in a French café but daren't take the religion or politics route, discussing French culinary pre-eminence and the Michelin and Gault Millau rating systems will do the trick. Just say, 'Did you realise that eleven of the world's twenty top restaurants are in London?', or, 'Don't you think it's crazy that Alain Senderens gave back his three stars one year and was then given two the next?', then sit back and rest your vocal chords.

For Paul Bocuse, Alain Ducasse, Joël Robuchon, Marc Veyrat, Pierre Gagnaire *et al* are more than cooks. They are living monuments to a glorious age and, to many, proof of their continuing world domination in culinary taste, creativity, daring and success. Unlike world-famous French politicians, artists, designers or film stars, they seem to object to vying for their place in a common international arena. French chefs carry on their shoulders the weighty heritage of François Vatel, Marie-Antoine Carême and Auguste Escoffier – an important part of France's grandeur.

Intellectual impetus from great French chefs and writers has shaped modern cooking throughout the world. Carême's theories on presentation and Escoffier's on structure, tomes from La Varenne, Alexandre Dumas, de la Raynière and Brillat-Savarin, have formed an important part of chefs' training worldwide. It was hardly surprising then, that Alain Ducasse caused a national outrage five years ago when he declared in *Gault Millau* magazine that French cuisine had lost its international prestige. An article in the *New York Times* reiterated the claim, causing an even greater scandal and fuelling a quiet revolution that has produced some exciting young chefs. They are more than ever grounded in the excellence of national produce, and many trained in Ducasse's schools, yet they are also influenced by Japanese, Californian and Australian food, and by Spanish chef Ferran Adrià's 'molecular gastronomy' (which uses chemistry and physics to spectacularly transform flavours and textures). These young chefs are currently morphing French cooking into a new artistic, metaphysical form. Important gastro-intellectual movements such as Le Fooding ® are helping to discover, define and federate the next generation.

Its most iconic member, Inaki Aizpitarte, is an imposing and charismatic figure; thirty-four years old, originally from the Basque country, 6 foot 3 inches and taciturn. In only five years he has taken on and elevated to cult status three separate restaurants: La Famille in Paris's Montmartre district, the Transversal in Vitry's contemporary art museum, and now his very own place in Paris, the furiously fashionable-without-trying Châteaubriand. His cooking heralds a new rebellious confidence and individual creativity freely fed by trends from other countries. Inaki, like many of the younger generation, does not feel shackled by the heavy legacy of France's culinary past. He has travelled all over the world and describes his cooking as 'cuisine vagabonde'. His ground-breaking dishes favour ingredients with strong personalities, cooked simply and presented beautifully. His aim is to have these strong and simple elements 'collide' with each other, moving the dish to a different taste level. He doesn't give a hoot about being one of France's rising stars. His piercing dark eyes flash with contempt when I suggest he could be France's equivalent to Jamie Oliver. 'Never! And don't say I'm a rock star either!'

This is typical of the strange anti-star trend, an embarrassment about media attention and publicised financial success. It is extremely important to the chefs that they be respected for their originality and be seen to be doing their jobs for reasons other than to become famous or make a lot of money. This reflects not only France's simultaneously socialist and conservative collective soul, but also the fact that chefs have always played an important role in the structure of French society and they see their work at times as vocational, a service to the community.

Superchef and international business tycoon Alain Ducasse is often criticised for being interested only in *le business*, and much of it outside France. Chefs who open businesses abroad, such as both Joël Robuchon and Guy Savoy in Las Vegas, are keeping very quiet about it in Paris. By contrast, in the UK Gordon Ramsay's growing international empire is hailed as a mini national glory. In France, every time a starred restaurant goes into receivership, more blame is attached to the public's lack of support and understanding of a national treasure than to the chef's lack of business acumen.

A French chef will greet with caution being described as a 'celebrity'. At the top end of the scale, chefs' achievement is measured by the extent of their creativity and innovation, and is judged by a handful of powerful critics rather than by level of economic success. It seems that worthy success must result from a combination of innate talent, hard toil, luck, respect for and attachment to a *terroir* (region), and even adherence to a spiritual value – as long as it is not seen to be money.

Superstar chef, Thierry Marx, is admired not only for his spectacularly poetic cooking (which fills his restaurant's tables months ahead), but also because he does it for free in street festivals, is a vegetarian, a humanist and a black belt in judo, and spends four months of every year 'living simply' in Japan. In a similar way to other famous French chefs, he has been interviewed on the main national news and profiled in *Le Monde* newspaper. He is perceived as a serious national commentator, not a potential primetime TV show host.

Cooking has therefore not become a significant contributor to the entertainment industry and, for the moment anyway, nothing indicates it ever will. Most home cooks do not learn from chefs by watching them cooking on TV. Only one food cable channel exists, and it draws consistently small audiences.

One chef whose signature dishes and unique style have made an impact on domestic cooking is Alain Passard, who caused a huge storm when, during the BSE crisis, he renounced his meat-roasting roots and created a menu based entirely on vegetables. Suddenly tomatoes became dessert and everyone rediscovered the true taste of carrots. When Alain Ducasse reinvented the famous bistro Aux Lyonnais and

La purée de Robuchon

Joël Robuchon's potato purée

It must be proof of how much thought and love the French put into their food that multi-starred chef Joël Robuchon's most famous dish is one of the simplest that exist: mashed potatoes. Just as with Michel Bras' *coulant au chocolat*, everyone knows that the secret is out yet everyone still dreams of eating the real thing made by the real chefs in their real restaurants.

I still vividly remember tasting Robuchon's babyfood-smooth purée during my first ever three-Michelin star meal. And no matter how much I still prefer salty Irish butter half melted in the crater of an Irish blue potato volcano, the nutty taste has stayed with me. It is ritually served at his Atelier Joël Robuchon in Paris whether you order it or not. But believe me, you won't send it back unfinished.

FOR 4–5

1kg waxy potatoes
250g very good unsalted butter, cold,
    cut into cubes
250ml hot full-fat milk
Salt and freshly ground black pepper

The original recipe calls for 'rattes', firm, maggot-shaped, waxy potatoes not usually preferred for foamier purées. They are cooked whole, then peeled, then put through the fine mesh of a vegetable grinder. Then they are dried slightly in a saucepan for 5 minutes, stirred all the while with a wooden spoon.

Next, the cold butter is mixed in a little at a time, again with a wooden spoon, making the purée smooth and unctuous. Finally hot milk is whisked in with a hand whisk, giving the purée an airiness before it is served immediately.

You could certainly leave out the 5-minute dry, or the vegetable mill and use a masher – but never use a blender or everything goes elastic. The most important element of the recipe to have filtered into French homes is the potato/butter ratio. An urban cooking myth had the ratio of 1kg of potato to 1kg of butter for a while, and even if Robuchon himself doesn't go to such lengths, suddenly everyone started to rethink not only the types of potatoes they were serving but how much butter went into them. It had also been accepted that you did milk or butter, but not both. Now some of my friends even add egg yolks to up the cholesterol even more.

Very often, a home-cooked version will end up as *rattes écrasées au beurre*, simply crushed ratte potatoes. Much kinder on those who lack technique, equipment or a sense of timing.

La tomate aux douze saveurs d'Alain Passard

Alain Passard's twelve-flavoured tomatoes

Passard's most famous dish, *tomate confite aux douze saveurs* was created in 1986 and helped him win his first Michelin star. He varied the theme over the years, moving from the slowly caramelised *tomate confite* to this chunkier stuffed version.

FOR 4

4 small tomatoes

1 tablespoon shelled walnuts

1 tablespoon shelled pistachios

1 tablespoon blanched shelled almonds

1 cm piece of fresh ginger, peeled

Zest and juice of 1 orange

Zest of 1 lemon

2–3 tablespoons sugar

2 apples, peeled, cored and chopped

2 pears, peeled, cored and roughly chopped

100 g fresh pineapple, peeled, cored and roughly copped

Pinch of cinnamon

3 cloves

1 vanilla pod

1 tablespoon sultanas

1 tablespoon chopped fresh mint

Preheat the oven to 200°C/400°F/gas mark 6.

Slice off the tops of the tomatoes, retaining their stalks. Bring a small pan of water to the boil then remove from the heat and plunge the bottom part of the tomatoes in for 1 minute. Remove their skin then remove the pips, juice and water from the inside.

Whizz together the nuts, ginger and both types of zest in a food-processor.

In a heavy-based pan, caramelise a little sugar (see page 142) then throw in the apples, pears and pineapple and cook for a minute or so. Slit the vanilla pod lengthways and scrape the seeds onto the fruit. Add the whizzed nut mixture and then all the remaining ingredients except for the orange juice and the remaining sugar. Mix well.

Stuff the tomatoes with the mixture and set the 'hats' on top.

In an ovenproof pan, make a caramel with the remaining sugar, add the orange juice (it will spit and splutter, be careful) and set the tomatoes in the caramel. Put the pan in the oven and roast the tomatoes for 5–8 minutes until the tomatoes soften and the fruit bubbles. Baste them with the orange caramel as often as possible.

Remove from the oven, leave to cool a little, then serve with vanilla ice cream.

south-western chef Yves Camdeborde set up the rustic bistro La Régalade in a far corner of Paris, both restaurants became feted by fim stars and politicians alike, and Alain and Yves led the way for a tidal wave of simple, hearty French dishes. Chic Parisian hostesses started serving *pot au feu* and *tarte tatin* at dinner, but flavoured with Moroccan spices and served in individual portions.

Trends started in the starry heights have influenced menus in smaller restaurants and filtered down into ready-prepared dishes sold in supermarkets and at the *traiteur*. Special or new ingredients made famous in chefs' signature dishes appeared in the shops and *épiceries fines*, and the restaurant dish or elements of it eventually come into the home. Every so often, a chef's signature dish will become so famous that everyone starts eating versions of it in lesser restaurants and friends' dinner tables. For instance, Joël Robuchon's potato purée suddenly had the French weighing out as much butter as potatoes before they got mashing. Michel Bras patented the recipe for his *coulant au chocolat*, from which a molten heart of chocolat sauce pours out as you break the warm outer biscuit, but it didn't stop a wave of replicas sweeping the country, and even from appearing in the Picard frozen food shops – now available in two sizes, *classique* and *mini*!

Our French home cook will use her talent to actively replicate what she has eaten in restaurants, even in the less starry kitchens. It is perfectly acceptable, while dining out, to ask how a dish has been cooked, where an ingredient was found or how a presentation technique was achieved. Most chefs are delighted to sense such interest from their clients and share their knowledge as happily as they jealously guard secrets from their counterparts. Having enjoyed and partially decoded a dish in a restaurant, the home cook will use the information and inspiration to produce her own creation, just as the couture collections provide a starting point for what our Française will be wearing as she serves dinner to her guests.

This is what I have tried to show in the recipes in this chapter. They are based on dishes I have tasted in restaurants and adapted to my own kitchen and skills.

Inaki

Pictured centre, surrounded by his team, Inaki Aizpitarte's impact on home cooking is just starting to be felt. His is a quest for simplification in the technique and complexity of a dish combined with more demanding expectations of the quality and intrinsic flavour of ingredients. He is in sync with the change of attitude and style of an entire generation, the first who didn't learn to cook by watching maman. Suddenly it is acceptable to mix lychees and mackerel, buttermilk and rose-scented sorbet, oysters and red fruits, as long as the flavours and technique are pure and simple and the ingredients of highest quality.

Ceviche de maquereaux et lychees

Mackerel and mustard ceviche with lychee sorbet

As heavenly as it sounds unlikely.

FOR 4

About 20 lychees, peeled and stoned (avoid tinned lychees at all costs), or the best-quality sorbet you can find

8 fresh mackerel fillets, cut into strips

Juice of 3 limes

1 tablespoon finely chopped chives or spring onions

Fleur de sel (sea salt)

Freshly ground black pepper

Purée the lychees and, if you don't have an ice-cream maker, freeze the purée in a Tupperware box, stirring every hour or so to break up the crystals.

Toss the mackerel strips with the lime juice and the chopped chives. Season with salt and pepper and leave to marinate in the fridge for at least 1 hour, and up to 5 hours.

Serve with some salad leaves, fresh coriander, Dijon mustard alongside and a scoop of sorbet on top.

Compote de pommes, beurre noisette

Apple compote and beurre noisette

The aim with this dessert is to cook the best apples in the simplest way – in France I would use Boskoop or Granny Smith, which are firm and slightly tart, and a far cry from astringent 'cookers'. The texture of Inaki's compote should be melting, *fondant*, and not puréed as is usually the case in France. In fact this is pretty much the way my mother served 'stewed' apples when I was a child. Try to cook quickly and lightly, leaving a little bite in the apples.

FOR 4

4–5 good-sized aromatic apples

A squeeze of lemon juice

2–3 tablespoons sugar

150 g (yes, really) of extremely good salted butter

Peel, core and cut the apples into 2–3 cm chunks. Put them in a heavy-based saucepan with a few splashes of water and the lemon juice, cover and cook for 10–15 minutes. The idea is to build up the steam and stew the apples in their own juice. Stir them a few times to make sure they don't stick to the pan. Add a little more water if need be, and sugar to taste.

When they are ready, remove them from the heat and spoon them into individual bowls.

In a frying pan, melt the butter, then continue heating it for a few minutes until it turns a nut-brown colour. This is 'noisette'. Pour it onto the apples, let it cool a little and serve.

Veau, compote de rhubarbe et oignons rouges

Veal with rhubarb and red onion compote and smoked lardons

Inaki's original recipe involved foul-smelling smoked fish eggs, as well as the most delicately pickled pink shallots, and beautiful deep purple, hazelnut-flavoured *vitelotte* potatoes. This domesticated-down version uses lardons for the smokiness, rhubarb for the pickledness and plain new potatoes to avoid the frustrating search for the elusive *vitelotte*, especially out of season (December to February).

This is very much a prepare-at-the-last-minute dish. You can make the compote beforehand, but for the rest you really will be playing chefs in front of your diners.

FOR 4

Olive oil, for frying

2 medium red onions, sliced

2–3 stalks pink rhubarb

8–10 new potatoes, scrubbed (or peeled if you can be bothered)

A small handful of smoked lardons, or thickly cut smoked bacon or *poitrine fumée* cut into chunks

4 nice chunks or slices of veal fillet, or 4 small veal cutlets, about 120 g each

1 tablespoon good curry powder, or a mild curried barbecue rub

75 g good butter

Fleur de sel (sea salt)

Ground white pepper

Start by making the red onion compote. In a heavy-based saucepan, heat a little olive oil and add the sliced onions. Cook down very gently for 5 minutes or so – you don't want them to fry or colour. When they start to soften, add the rhubarb and a splash of water. Cover the pan and let the compote cook slowly for a further 5–10 minutes. Season with *fleur de sel* and pepper and leave to cool.

Boil some water in a pan and put the potatoes in it to cook. Try to have them hot and ready to crush when the veal is cooked; they can be heated up again in the microwave if necessary.

Heat a heavy-based frying pan and throw in the lardons – there is no need to add oil or butter. When they are golden and crispy, turn them onto some kitchen paper to mop up any excess fat and keep them warm.

Wipe the pan clean if there are any burnt bits in it; if not, make the most of the smoky, salty residue. Just let the pan cool down a little, then pour in a splash of olive oil.

Heat the oil and fry the veal. Start by browning it on all sides, then reduce the heat and let the meat cook through. Sprinkle it with the curry powder and turn it around a few times in the pan to seal the powder onto the outside of the meat and form a very light crust.

Crush the cooked potatoes with the butter and spoon them onto individual plates. Balance the veal on top, sprinkle with lardons and serve with the compote.

Gateau au chocolat à la fleur de sel et huile d'olive

Chocolate cake with olive oil and salt

Chocolate has been daringly teamed with many unexpected flavours, from roquefort in Jean Paul Hévin's ganache to wood in the *bûche de Noel* designed by Philippe Starck. It was Pierre Hermé who made adding salt to chocolate (milk at first) popular. Here Inaki takes things one step further with the addition of olive oil. Surprisingly, it works. The olive oil smoothes the palette, thus enhancing the depth of the bitter chocolate's aromas. And the crunch of the *fleur de sel* brings out its sweetness.

FOR 8

200g best-quality dark chocolate, minimum 70% cocoa solids

200g unsalted butter

4 medium eggs

150g caster sugar

60g plain flour

1¹⁄₂ teaspoons baking powder

Extra virgin olive oil

Fleur de sel (sea salt)

Preheat the oven to 200°C/400°F/gas mark 6. Grease and flour a 22cm sandwich tin.

Melt the chocolate and the butter together in short blasts and stirs in the microwave, or more sedately in a bain-marie (see page 219). Stir with a wooden spoon to mix the two ingredients completely.

Put the eggs and the sugar in a bowl and whisk with electric beaters until the mixture turns pale and doubles in volume. Add the flour, a tablespoonful at a time, and the baking powder.

Mix in the chocolate mixture, pour the lot into the prepared sandwich tin and bake for 20–25 minutes. The cake is cooked when a knife inserted into the centre comes out clean.

Leave the cake to cool for 15 minutes before turning out. Ideally, you should wait till the next day before serving it – chocolate cakes are always better when they have settled down a little, and in this case, where we are concentrating on pure and simple flavours, it is even more advisable.

To serve, cut the cake into slices, set them on plain white plates and pour some extra virgin olive oil around. Serve with some *fleur de sel* (on the side, for the timorous and the dubious).

It is very disconcerting to see the slice of chocolate cake, which on the menu is called simply 'gâteau au chocolat maison', turn up surrounded by olive oil and served with fleur de sel. But Inaki's combination is wonderful.

Ducasse

In the 1980s Alain Ducasse's deceptively simple, intense Mediterranean cooking at his restaurant in Monaco was largely responsible for the surge in popularity in Provençal food and olive oil. His lighter, aromatic *jus*, both meat- and vegetable-based, heralded the end of the traditional *demi glace* so popular before the arrival of *nouvelle cuisine*. Sauces no longer required bone braising and boiling for hours, and the home cook breathed a sigh of relief as the new approach allowed her to leave her stockpot in the cupboard.

Ducasse was the first starred chef who dared use industrially produced cult brands as ingredients in his dishes at his Parisian ground-breaking restaurant, Spoon. *Fraises tagada* (see opposite), for example, are wild-strawberry-flavoured impossibly pink sweets that every French person will have tasted. The instant nostalgic pleasure, the singular familiarity of their taste, no matter how chemically produced it may be, gave Ducasse justification enough to use them to make ice cream served alongside more classically created desserts.

Pizza au chocolat   Chocolate pizza

FOR 6

1 ready-made round pizza base
Dark chocolate spread, or Nutella if you really can't find anything else
Dried and sugared fruit (candied orange peel, dates, candied pineapple...)
Fresh fruit (clementines, pineapple, apple...)
Pine nuts, toasted

Preheat the oven to 200°C/400°F/gas mark 6.

Unroll the pizza base onto a baking tray and cook it for about 5 minutes until it starts to crisp up.

Remove from the oven and spread with chocolate. Dot the candied and fresh fruit over the pizza. Sprinkle with pine nuts and return to the oven for a further 5 minutes until the chocolate and fruit are hot. Serve the pizza straight from the oven.

Glace aux fraises tagada

Fraise tagada ice cream

This home-made recipe for a basic custard-based ice cream simply uses the bubblegum sweetness and colour of the tagada to flavour the custard. Certainly more or less the way it is done at Spoon! You will need to use an ice-cream maker.

FOR 6

6 egg yolks
1 tablespoon sugar
500g full-fat milk
300g Fraises tagada, plus extra
 for sprinkling

In a large bowl, beat together the egg yolks and the sugar. Bring the milk to the boil and pour it onto the eggs and sugar, mixing vigorously.

Pour the custard into a pan and return it to a medium heat, stirring continuously, and cook until it thickens enough to coat the back of a wooden spoon. Do not let it boil or heat too much at the bottom of the saucepan or it will curdle.

When the custard has thickened, remove it from the heat and add the *Fraises tagada*, stirring until they have completely dissolved. Let the custard cool completely before churning it in an ice-cream maker.

Serve with real strawberries and a few more *tagada*!

Sardines à la tapenade, tomates séchées et roquette

Sardines with tapenade, sun-dried tomatoes and rocket

**Along with the Costes brothers' *tomates mozzarella basilic* (caprèse salad),
Alain Ducasse was largely responsible for the wave of Italian/Provençal dishes and
ingredients that swept France in the 1990s. Suddenly tapenade and anchoiade were
everywhere, rocket had dethroned *mâche* (lambs' lettuce) and sun-dried tomatoes
invaded just as they did the UK. The combination of these star ingredients with
lightly grilled or barbecued sardines is wonderful. Add a thin slice of toasted Poilâne
bread or olive-soaked fougasse for the full Mediterranean experience.**

FOR 4

4–6 fresh sardines
4–6 sun-dried tomatoes in oil
3–4 handfuls of rocket leaves
Extra virgin olive oil
Salt and freshly ground black pepper

FOR THE TAPENADE
**About 25 pitted French olives
   (black or green)**
1 tablespoon drained capers
1 tablespoon lemon juice
2 tablespoons olive oil
1 garlic clove
2–3 anchovies in oil
Freshly ground black pepper

Put all the tapenade ingredients in a mini-blender and whizz for a minute or so, depending
on how chunky you like it.

Grill the sardines and serve with the tapenade, the sun-dried tomatoes and the rocket
drizzled with a little olive oil and seasoned with salt and pepper.

Darroze

Alain Ducasse's influence is also felt throughout the industry in the chefs he has trained. Hélène Darroze is one of them. She is a native of the south-western region of the Landes, where the Darroze family had reigned in their famous restaurant for many years. Hélène set up her own restaurant in Paris and quickly scooped up two Michelin stars and the limelight fell not only on Basque country cusine and south-west produce, but also on the woman herself. She is a tiny, fragile yet steely woman, fiercely proud of her achievement, brushing off the notion of machismo within the industry.

Her eponymous restaurant in the 5th arrondissement has dark wood floors, purple velvet on the walls and chairs that fold around the diner. Here you will feast on *poulet des landes*, ceps, foie gras and chocolate, cooked from the heart by Hélène. 'I never try to anticipate what my clients may like,' she declares. 'I cook what I like.' In the 'salon' and 'boudoir', state-of-the-art tapas and finger-food morsels are served set into plates specially designed by French designer Matali Grasset. Hélène's 'madeleine', normally a sweet cake, isn't sweet at all, it is a dish based entirely around foie gras.

Last year, Hélène published a remarkable best-selling cookery book, where the story of her dishes was intertwined with her own life, and notably a fiery and secretive love affair she had for many years with a prominent married man (who remains anonymous in the book but, as is typical in France, is known to many). The affair ended bitterly but Hélène's cooking didn't suffer; on the contrary, just as any other artist would, she used it. 'I was more in tune with my own feelings,' she says. 'I was able to dig deeper, create more, cook more sincerely than ever. It helped.' Not only has she made foie gras, piquillos and *piment d'espellette* more popular, she has also given many French women home cooks the confidence to allow their sensuality and feminity to shine through in a male-dominated gastronomic world.

Bloody Mary Basque

Basque country bloody mary

Hélène Darroze's version of the classic drink is made with fresh tomato juice.
Here I have simply liquidised, not juiced, the tomatoes with some ready-made
tomato juice and pimientos de piquillo to give a thicker consistency.

Put the tomato juice, tomatoes and piquillos in a liquidiser and whizz till smooth.

Chill well before serving with a good dash of vodka. Flavour with celery salt and
Worcestershire sauce if you wish, and a squeeze of lemon and ice cubes to serve.

FOR 2

300 ml good-quality fresh tomato juice
2 tomatoes, skinned
3–4 pimientos de piquillo (see
   page 94)
Vodka
Celery salt
Worcestershire sauce
Lemon
Ice cubes

Poulet des Landes farci aux coquillettes au foie gras

Landes country chicken stuffed with macaroni and foie gras

This is a pared-down version of one of Hélène Darroze's most famous dishes. I remember tasting it in her Parisian restaurant just two days before my daughter was born – perhaps that is why she loves roast chicken so much. It's the only roast chicken that has ever come close to beating my mother's.

FOR 6–8

1 excellent chicken (try to find a 'poulet jaune des Landes', corn-fed chicken from the Landes region; otherwise, use the best you can buy

Oil, butter or goose fat, for frying

2 whole garlic cloves

4 bay leaves

250 ml chicken stock

FOR THE STUFFING

500 g raw foie gras or, at a pinch, a good-quality terrine de foie gras, *mi-cuit* if possible.

400 g small macaroni pasta

1 bay leaf

1 tablespoon flat-leaf parsley

1 whole garlic clove

Olive oil

Salt and piment d'Espelette or freshly ground black pepper

Preheat the oven to 180°C/350°/gas mark 4.

If you are using raw foie gras in the stuffing, cut it into cubes, sprinkle it with salt and piment d'Espelette or pepper and toss it very quickly in a hot frying pan, just long enough to brown it on all sides. Drain it on some kitchen paper and set aside.

Put the macaroni in boiling water with the bay leaf and cook until just al dente. Drain and refresh with cold water to stop them cooking further. Discard the bay leaf and put the macaroni in a large bowl and mix with the foie gras, parsley and olive oil.

Stuff the chicken with the mixture and seal the cavity: sew it up, or use a hem stapler, or cover with a little aluminium foil.

Heat the oil, butter or goose fat in a roasting tin and brown the chicken all over. Add the garlic clove and the bay leaves to the pan, transfer to the oven and cook for about 50 minutes, basting regularly. Remove the chicken from the oven and let it rest for about 10 minutes.

Meanwhile, make the gravy. Heat the chicken stock in a saucepan. Get rid of the excess fat in the roasting tin then pour in the stock, scraping the residue from the bottom of the tin. Let it bubble and reduce on the hob for a few minutes.

Serve the chicken whole and carve it at the table accompanied by the gravy and any extra stuffing heated up in a little of the cooking juices.

Glace à la truffe noire

Black truffle ice cream

An excellent way of using those little jars of truffle juice and truffle shavings or of using eggs which have cohabited with a fresh truffle in your fridge. You will need an ice-cream maker for this recipe.

FOR 8

250 ml full-fat milk or single cream
20 g truffle juice
10 g truffle shavings
25 g sugar
2 egg yolks

Heat the milk or cream with the truffle juice and shavings.

In a pan, beat together the sugar and the egg yolks until the mixture is pale. Pour the hot milk into the mixture and stir. Heat the mixture gently until it thickens, stirring constantly. Do not let it boil or curdle at the base of the pan. Remove from the heat and leave to infuse and cool for 4–5 hours.

Churn in an ice-cream maker and serve immediately with a very bitter dark chocolate sauce or plain dense chocolate cake.

Chocolat chaud au piment d'Espelette et à la vanille

Hot chocolate with Espelette pepper and vanilla

Shades of Joanne Harris here as the Basque hot pepper spices up an unctuous hot chocolate. This is such a simple recipe, I have hardly changed it at all.

FOR 4

250 ml full-fat milk

250 ml single cream

1 vanilla pod, split lengthways

Espelette pepper, or chilli pepper if you don't have the Basque equivalent

150 g dark chocolate (around 60% cocoa solids), finely grated

Bring the milk and the cream to the boil in a saucepan then remove from the heat.

Scrape the seeds from the vanilla pod and add both the pod and the seeds to the milk and cream, along with a pinch of pepper. Leave to infuse for 5 minutes or so.

Pour the creamy milk onto the chocolate and mix gently with a small hand whisk until the chocolate is completely melted.

Heat the chocolate milk again, very gently, without boiling, like a custard. It will become even creamier. Serve immediately, with a tiny dusting of Espelette pepper on top.

chapter 4

rises to the occasion

When the French entertain it is usually with seemingly effortless flair –
huge expense or sophistication are never prerequisites for successful
meals. Whether the simplest outdoor lunch, elaborate dinner or a rowdy
party, it's the care taken, the planning, the confidence and anticipated
pleasure that infuse the meal with magic. The cooks who have instilled
some of these aspects in my cooking over the years are those who
opened their homes and hearts and kitchens. Of my mother's generation,
all of them cook and entertain constantly and brilliantly. We can learn a
lot from them.

The first and most influential of my domestic mentors and an example of how French cooks rise to the occasion every time, is Louisette Vezin, who took me in when I was 18 after a summer job went very wrong in La Roche sur Yon, Vendée. Her first comforting gesture was also a true rite of passage. I was very shy and my French was not wonderful. She sat me at her kitchen table before an enormous pile of sweet, steamed langoustines with parsley and her peppery, eggy mayonnaise and at once we had found a common language. To my fascination, Louisette would cook three courses for lunch and dinner every day and would hold dinner parties, lunches or barbecues at least three times in any week, with 'walk-ins' encouraged.

Louisette shopped like a whirlwind. Every day she would devise her lunchtime and often evening menus in the time it took her to sweep through the market. One hour before lunch must be on the table, in 20 minutes and five stops, *le tour est fait.* Cheese, fish, fruit and vegetables, charcuterie and beef. Extremely fickle in her choice of seller, with the exception of fish, she gauged the queue/quality balance at every stall. No queue? Nothing interesting. Too large a queue? Not worth waiting. She visited the large covered market in the centre of La Roche every day and always kept her freezer and cupboards ingeniously stocked with special things that would eke out any meal or transform a starter to main and vice versa.

When she cooked, unless I asked a specific question, Louisette never described what she was doing. We always had too many other subjects to discuss and there was no need for demo-chef banter as she peeled or crushed or sliced. All I had to do was watch, and later, eat, to understand how vital to the quality of the food these repetitive yet highly skilled tasks were. But what Louisette conveyed was the opposite of drudgery. It was a spectacular show she didn't realise she was giving and for which she turned in the same performance regardless of who her audience would be. She was driven along by the pleasure she derived from meeting her own exacting standards and the promise of what her guests would invariably experience upon consuming her food.

From her I learned the art of balancing menus, never repeating an ingredient or conversely, including it in different forms at every course as the meal's thread or *fil conducteur*, keeping other dishes light if the main course is particularly filling or has a rich sauce. She taught me the importance of good stock, how to reduce and caramelise, how to sweat garlic and shallots and the consequences of them burning, how to brown and deglaze meat, how not to overcook fish, how to serve a simple salad and vinaigrette, how to put together a cheeseboard.

Louisette rarely cooked puddings, and therefore had an impressive list of sweet suppliers – *pâtissiers*, *chocolatiers* or ice-cream makers. That summer we often made the hour-long trip to Nantes, the car full of insulating boxes ready to house spectacular ice-cream cakes from the best *glacier* in town. Her tables were always pretty. Even at family lunchtimes the crockery and napkins matched the red checked wallpaper. And when the entertaining took place on the outside terrace or in the large sitting room cum library, candles, flowers and linen tablecloths always appeared.

As we toured around visiting friends and relatives I discovered the reality of the fabled four-hour French lunch. Parties for birthdays, retirements or engagements were sumptuous affairs. Held in gardens, on the beach, in garages, on boats or in stables they were lavish, always seamless, jolly and cheerfully drunken. Never was the notion of chore or useless hard work attached to these occasions. For Louisette and so many cooks I have met over my years in France, entertaining well is a natural, generous and pleasurable part of everyone's existence, and remains right at the core of family and social lives.

Southern living
Languedoc

Patric and Greg spend their summers in an imposing stone house in the tiny village of Pailhes. Just ten kilometres from the city of Béziers (which was once the beating heart of the entire Languedoc region), the house is provincial-Bourgeois in style and the decor is a mixture of old and new: large gilt mirror, groaning *armoires*, vast desks and ancient beds stand alongside recently bought *brocante* and pieces from IKEA. Posters and paintings of the *corrida* abound, and the kitchen, all red and yellow, is themed around Spain. It's a two-hour drive to the border and the Iberian influence is found in the food everywhere between Nîmes and Perpignan.

In Patric's family for generations, the house was previously used by his wine-producing grandfather as a base during the *vendange* (grape harvest). Scores of migrant grape-pickers would toil all day in the vineyards and enjoy rowdy communal meals set out on long trestle tables in the same fields at night. It resembled something out of Marcel Pagnol.

Half of the third floor of the house was recently removed to create a terrace where evening meals and parties take place. Lanterns, fairy lights, torches and candles illuminate the space at night. The terrace overlooks rolling vineyards stretching towards Béziers' floodlit Cathédrale St-Nazaire in the east and the Montagne Noir in the west. The Languedoc has it all – rivers, the sea and fascinating villages like St-Guilherm-le-Désert, historic towns like Carcasonne and Pézenas, the Parc Naturel Régional, romantic Cathar castles and the Camargue and Provence are just a stone's throw away.

The Feria de Béziers in August is a four-day festival of bull-fighting and hedonism which revivifies the city annually. The town becomes one great *bodega* with locals selling rosé and tapas from street stalls. For the Feria weekend Greg will cook an enormous paella or *garde de taureau*, preceded by local olives and gazpacho (red and white) – all followed by local cheeses like rocquefort. For smaller meals he'll cook *saucisse de Toulouse* and *côtes d'agneau* in the kitchen's open hearth – using vine stumps for fuel. The wines of the region are great – even the *vin de table* (Faugères and Les Corbières are just a stone's throw away). The local muscat is sensational.

There are no shops in Pailhes – just a small pizzeria from which you can order some of the best pizzas I've ever tasted; crispy, thin bases with inventive toppings like crème fraîche, the juiciest grilled pears, runny lavender honey and fragrant toasted almonds.

Gaspacho blanc White gazpacho

Everyone knows red gazpacho, but the white version – ajo blanco – is less ubiquitous but equally delicious and refreshing. You could even serve red and white gazpachos together (in separate receptacles, of course). The following recipe is somewhat approximate, as it is based on the ingredients listed on the back of a shop-bought version. It works though.

FOR 4 (photographed opposite, left)

200g good-quality blanched almonds
750ml iced water
4–5 slices stale white bread with crusts removed – soaked in water
4 garlic cloves
3 tablespoons extra virgin olive oil
3 tablespoons sherry vinegar
Fleur de sel (sea salt)
Ground white pepper

In a food-processor, grind the almonds as finely as possible. Add one cup of the water, then squeeze the bread and add to the almonds with the garlic. With the machine running, add more water, the olive oil and the vinegar. Taste. There should be a pleasant balance between the almonds, garlic and vinegar. If the balance isn't to your liking, add more of any of the above ingredients. When you are happy with the flavour, chill for a few hours, taste again (adjust seasoning) and serve with halved, seedless white grapes.

You could also garnish the soup with small chunks of cucumber and mint, flat-leaf parsley, chopped hard-boiled egg, snipped chives and/or toasted flaked almonds.

Sangria blanche White sangria

Sangria is redolent of student days where a few bottles of red wine and whatever hard liquor was lying around were pressed into service (with some over-ripe fruit).

**White Sangria is cleaner looking and tasting, and altogether more elegant...
Greg and Patric use only citrus fruit as apples, peaches etc. tend to discolour.
This Sangria takes about 5 to 10 minutes to assemble, but prepare it in the morning so the mixture has several hours to develop its tangy flavour.**

MAKES 8 TALL GLASSES (photographed opposite, right)

4 tablespoons sugar
2 limes, sliced
2 lemons, sliced
2 oranges, sliced
1 bottle of cheap dry white wine
1 litre of sparkling soda water

Combine the sugar, limes, lemons and oranges in a large bowl. Cover with 1 bottle of dry white wine and chill for several hours. Serve this sangria from a tall, undecorated glass pitcher or jug into tall, undecorated chilled glasses. Add sparkling soda water to the wine and fruit mixture once you've transferred it to the serving jug. Taste (add more sugar if necessary) and serve.

Play with the recipe as you see fit. Instead of soda, you could add a mixture of bitter lemon and soda – or even just lemonade. Add Cointreau and Limoncello to augment the citrus and alcohol quotient. Remember, however, to taste as you proceed.

This is an invention that bypasses the admittedly simple preparations for the Catalan classic 'Pan con tomate'. *Pan con tomate* (shown in the photograph above right) involves toasting thick slabs of country bread over (ideally) a wood fire until lightly golden. The bread is rubbed with garlic, then tomato halves, and drizzled with olive oil, and sprinkled with coarse salt and freshly ground black pepper. To save time and effort, put two tomatoes, two garlic cloves, *fleur de sel*, coarse pepper and extra virgin olive oil in a blender and whizz for a couple of seconds. Taste to see if the mixture is sufficiently fruity. If not, add a little sugar or honey (too much and you'll need to add more salt). Add a few basil leaves if you like and whizz once more. Turn out into a bowl and serve with bread or crudités for breakfast, lunch, or as a tapa prior to the evening meal. If you are keeping the mush in the fridge, the garlic flavour is likely to augment. Adjust seasoning before serving. Equally good as a light sauce for fish.

'Gratin de figues'

A delicious and easy way to use the figs that litter the roads of the Languedoc come late August. Allow at least two figs per person. Slice off the stem of each fig. Cut the figs in half lengthways, then place them, cut side up, in a shallow oven-proof dish. Place half a teaspoon of honey on each fig half and squeeze a few drops of lemon juice over them, then sprinkle some ground almonds and dollop all over with butter. Bake for about 15 minutes. The juice from the figs and the honey should form a syrup and the butter will make it all deliciously creamy. Leave to cool in the cooking dish before serving.

Aubergine à la Nimoise   Stuffed aubergine

1 large aubergine
2 tablespoons olive oil
1 medium onion, finely chopped
6 black olives in brine or vinegar
Handful of drained capers
Handful of parmesan cheese
2–3 garlic cloves, finely chopped
Handful of fresh white breadcrumbs
Parsley, chives, basil, pepper, salt
2 anchovies (optional)

Preheat the oven to 160°C/325°F/gas mark 3. Cut the aubergine in half lengthways. With a sharp knife make horizontal and vertical slashes through the flesh in a crisscross pattern, being careful not to pierce the skin. Work in lots of salt to draw out any bitterness. Set aside for 30 minutes. Rinse the aubergines and pat dry. Scoop out the squares you made when slashing the flesh. Heat the oil in a frying pan and fry the aubergine skins gently until golden brown. Remove from the pan, and place on a baking tray. Gently fry the onion until soft, then add the aubergine squares for a few minutes until they break down. Remove from the heat and mix in the rest of the ingredients (including the anchovies if using) and a few tablespoons of brine or vinegar from the olives. Spoon this mixture into the aubergine skins, pressing the filling down. Bake for 20 minutes until the stuffing is crisp on top.

Sépions à la plancha Pan-fried cuttlefish

Cuttlefish (*seiche* in French) is often mistaken for calamari or squid. It has short-ish tentacles and a comparatively large body, and is distinguished by the calcified cartilage so loved by budgies. In my view, cuttlefish has more flavour than its cousins, and its ink sacs are prized in Italian, Spanish and Croatian cuisine. That said, no matter how carefully it's cooked, this mollusc has an undeniable chewiness that some people find offputting. Personally, I adore the simplicity of quickly fried cuttlefish.

FOR 4

4 sepia
8 garlic cloves
Bunch of flat-leaf parsley
Salt
Pepper
Olive oil

Buy it cleaned by your fishmonger, although cleaning them at home is child's play – just remember, you want to be left with the translucent white body and tentacles, so discard everything else. Most recipes tell you to cut it into strips, but I prefer throwing it on to a *plancha* (although a frying pan will do) and watching it retract on contact with the heat. While waiting for it to cook (5 minutes on each side should do nicely), make a *persillade* – which is just minced garlic and parsley, a little salt, cracked pepper and lashings of good olive oil. Pour this mixture over the plated cuttlefish, and serve with a wedge of lemon and some plain boiled rice.

Parisian bobo style

Lou's home is snuggled in an old crumbling building in Paris's 9th arrondissement. A scriptwriter and film director, Lou's poetic and ultra-refined dinners are conceived and concocted in much the same way as her stories and films. To inspire her cooking, Lou defines a theme, and then lets it run through the entire occasion. The set is invariably her kitchen library, the props are the flowers and china, and the costumes are carefully chosen outfits. Lou loves to be surrounded by what she calls her *fleurs de compagnie*, or 'pet flowers', so it seemed obvious that this early June dinner would take a floral theme. Lou's first shopping stop, before even considering the menu, was at 8am at her favourite flower shop.

The food was picked up in the course of the morning, in the 9th and 10th arrondissements, at Lou's favourite suppliers. She is extremely demanding of them. For her, the quality of the produce should shine through in every meal, and her recipes are anything but sophisticated. She buys fresh pasta, an array of fresh spring vegetables, swordfish and pink peaches, making up her menu as she goes along. Lou describes her dinners as '*mises en danger*', calculated risks, as she feels compelled to make up new recipes every time she entertains. The possibility of failure adds sharply to the pleasure she derives from creating something new and unexpected.

Already thinking of how she will dress, and of which dishes and cutlery she will use from her impressive collection, (mainly nineteenth century, with many pieces from the UK), Lou sets to work. The aperitif requires only a little chopping and arranging; she prepares a simple spread of fresh cherries, pears, parmesan and grissini breadsticks, served with a Meursault 2001 brought along by her neighbour and fellow film director (see photograph on page 1).

For the *salade primavera*, inspired by one she tasted in a Rome restaurant, Lou throws together a variety of spring vegetables, raw or cold, with piping hot pasta that draws out their flavour in the heat. The Sicilian swordfish, a recipe copied from friends in Stromboli, is twice cooked in a lemon and garlic paste, and served with a salad of white beans or fagioli and raw celery. Lou doesn't go in for puddings, so she rarely cooks cakes or pastry, preferring fresh fruit in a salad, or poached and served with shop-bought meringues or macaroons. This time, she simply ends off the floral theme by poaching her ripe peaches in water with a touch of rosewater and decorating them with the petals of the old roses she found that morning *chez* Garance.

Soupe de pêches aux petales de roses

Peach soup with rose petals

FOR 8

8 plump, ripe flavoursome peaches
Rosewater or rosewater syrup
Petals from untreated roses

To poach the peaches, place them whole in a large pan, fill the pan about halfway up the side of the peaches and cover, then cook in simmering water for 15 minutes. Peel them, cut in half and remove the stones.

Add a little rosewater or rosewater syrup to the cooking water and spoon it over the peaches, then leave to cool.

Serve sprinkled with the petals and accompanied by meringues.

Salade primavera

Primavera salad

This is Lou's seasonal but simple pasta salad (see photograph opposite, bottom left), using green vegetables are most fresh at the market that day.

FOR 8

150g broad beans, podded

12 green asparagus spears

8 courgette flowers

4 green courgettes

20 cherry tomatoes

200g buffalo mozzarella

A good handful of flat-leaf parsley

A good handful of basil leaves

Extra virgin olive oil

Balsamic vinegar

Salt

Freshly ground pepper

500g fresh pasta (penne or rigatoni, or similar)

In separate batches, steam the broad beans, asparagus and courgette flowers very lightly. They must remain firm. Chop the courgettes into bite-sized chunks and cut the tomatoes in half. Tear the mozzarella into pieces.

In a large salad bowl, mix the mozzarella, vegetables and herbs together with some olive oil, a dash of balsamic vinegar and some salt and pepper.

Cook the pasta until al dente, strain and throw immediately into the vegetables. Toss and serve immediately. The heat from the pasta helps the flavours to develop and mingle.

Poisson grillé à la Sicilienne

Sicilian swordfish

FOR 8

2 onions

1 unwaxed lemon

1 garlic clove

A handful of flat-leaf parsley

1 tablespoon olive oil

8 thin swordfish steaks (around 150–200g each)

Handful of capers

Salt and freshly ground black pepper

In a food-processor, whizz the onions, the whole lemon, the garlic, parsley and olive oil to a fine paste. Season lightly with salt and pepper.

In a large, very hot frying pan or on a plancha, and working in batches, seal the swordfish briefly on both sides. Remove from the pan, spread the lemon paste on the fish and cook again until golden and crispy. When ready, sprinkle over a handful of capers.

Serve with a salad of white beans mixed with finely chopped celery and olive oil.

Wild at heart
Normandy

Gerald's fisherman's cottage in Coutainville, a tiny village on the west coast of Normandy's Manche peninsula, was built from *pierres tout venant* (any old stones). He lined the empty shell of the house with long wooden planks and made the rooms flow into each other, just as in a long wooden boat. Gerald was born a few kilometres away in Coutances. A textile and interiors stylist, he divides his time between Paris, Africa and his Normandy haven. Here, he is surrounded on all sides by open country, the estuary or the sea (with a view of the 'exotic' Channel Islands in the distance) and the wild fragility of the region provides inspiration for his work and his cooking.

A prolific and pragmatic cook, Gerard entertains frenetically during the holidays, when the village is full of friends. He is a stickler for using only local ingredients but not overly obsessed with sourcing the finest suppliers. His cooking revolves around the ultra-fresh seafood, fish, apples, cider, cream and camembert that he purchases mainly at the local Franprix supermarket. Creativity is his credo, he detests repetition and loves the idea of using his guests as guinea pigs for his new ideas. The newly planted gigantic pots of fresh herbs outside the kitchen have opened even more new horizons for his inventions.

Setting the scene is important to Gerald: his cutlery and crockery are carefully and lovingly chosen. But he has long since abandoned last-minute preparation deemed too stressful. Now his gatherings are still simple, yet planned to the last detail. He serves the likes of chilled beetroot and buttermilk soup or warm nettle and cream velouté, simple lobster and pasta salad, whelks or mussels served cold with cream, curry and fresh herbs, and oysters with just about anything. Here they are simply given a turn under the grill with a little crème fraîche and nutmeg. Other variations include warm camembert and apples or cold with thin slivers of *andouille*, a local sausage made from tripe. Normandy is famous for its apples, and Gerald likes to prepare crumbles and the thinnest of thin apple pies, served with local dry cider for his friends from the Coutainville 'creative ghetto'.

Our late-summer dinner at Gerald's started al fresco amongst Gerald's palm trees and Japanese anemones, but as a storm broke, the contents of the carefully set table in the courtyard were hurriedly regrouped in the dining room. Gerald's eclectic collection of English silver, French ceramics and glass contrasts with the plain and simple local food. As an appetizer, he serves *crevettes grises*, grey prawns and *bigourneaux*, winkles, ready cooked from his local fishmonger. They are served simply *tel quel* (as they are), or sometimes with a little mayonnaise for dipping the winkles. The pink carafe is an early creation of the design team Robert le Héros, better known for their fabrics. The ebony and bone salad servers are French and the silver from a London flea market Gerald liked to visit when he lived near Earl's Court.

Fromage de chèvre à l'huile d'olive

Goat's cheese in olive oil

A favourite dish, served either before or after the main course, is local goat's cheese marinated in olive oil. Gerald simply lets them rest in his fridge, with a few peppercorns and a little salt, for 2–3 days before serving with fresh bread.

FOR 6

6 fresh goat's cheeses, about 50g each
Rosemary, thyme, sage
A garlic clove, peeled and crushed
2–3 peppercorns
Fleur de sel (sea salt)
500ml good-quality olive oil

Place the cheese in a large preserving jar, or a tall glass bowl with the herbs, garlic and peppercorns.

Pour over the olive oil to immerse the cheeses, close the jar with its lid or cover the bowl tightly with clingfilm and leave in the fridge for 3–4 days before serving.

Pinces de tourteaux mayonnaise

Crab's claws with saffron mayonnaise

Crab's claws, like the prawns and winkles, come ready prepared from Gerald's fishmonger. Thrown simply into a beautiful *feuille de chou* dish, (again found during his years in London) Gerald likes to serve them with a home-made mayonnaise flavoured with a pinch of saffron.

FOR 6

12 crab claws (defrosted or fresh)
Salt
A large jar of good-quality
shop-bought mayonnaise
A pinch of saffron

Bring a large saucepan of lightly salted water to the boil.

Plunge the crab claws into the water and simmer for 15 minutes. Leave them to cool before cracking open with nutcrackers and serving with saffron-flavoured mayonnaise.

Soupe froide de betteraves et lait ribot

Chilled beetroot and buttermilk soup

A refreshing summer soup, the tartness of the buttermilk contrasts nicely with the sweet beetroot and the colour is fabulous. Don't use beetroot cooked in vinegar.

FOR 8

2–3 beetroots, cooked
1 litre fresh buttermilk
Juice and zest of 2 limes
2–3 tablespoons chopped chives
Salt and freshly ground black pepper

Put the beetroots and the buttermilk in a food-processor and liquidize.

Stir in the lime juice and zest, and a little water if the soup is too thick. Season with salt and pepper, and chill until needed. Sprinkle with the chives just before serving.

Huîtres pour l'apéro   Oysters for aperitif

Gerald loves experimenting with different ways to serve local oysters. He often serves them warm, not with an intricate champagne sauce, but simply, with a little cream and nutmeg.

FOR 6

12 *fines de Claire* oysters

250g crème fraîche

2–3 slices of bacon, cut into strips and fried

¹/₂ camembert

1–2 apples, grated, peeled and cored

Freshly ground nutmeg

Rock salt

Preheat the grill, or the oven to 180°C/350°F/gas mark 4. Pour a thick layer of rock salt into the grill pan or baking tray.

Open the oysters and drain their water.

In a bowl, mix the crème fraîche with the remaining ingredients.

Settle the oysters in their half shells and top with the crème fraîche mixture. Set them firmly into the prepared tray and grill or roast in the oven for a few minutes, until the cream bubbles.

Serve immediately.

Un thé chez Hélène

The rough, ruddy walls studded with African art, dark wooden furniture and jungle-like balconies of Hélène's Parisian courtyard apartment reflect her enduring love for Morocco. As a child she spent many magical holidays at her grandparents' home in Marrakesh, cosseted by her beloved Moroccan *fatma* who smelled of 'flour, yeast and warm, smooth bread'. From her, she learned the importance of cooking rituals, how precious it is to spend time and care executing the simplest gestures, and the value of keeping traditions alive through sharing them day after day.

Hélène's Sunday four o'clock teatime gathering has now become a ritual in itself. Friends arrive after visiting an exhibition or before going to the cinema, relaxed, full of news, gossip and opinions, keen to ignore usual meal times and stave off Monday-morning blues. Conversation is always lively, Hélène's crowd are artists, stylists, designers and journalists; many of them live nearby in this dense and noisy neighbourhood, which is still referred to as 'la nouvelle Athènes'. This name it earned in the nineteenth century when painters and poets set up their studios in the narrow streets around the Place Saint George, nestled between Montmartre and the theatres of the Grands Boulevards.

An obsessive consumer of cookery books, Hélène will tell you she has 'zero imagination' and 'an indomitable taste for risk', which combined have her pouring over her kitchen library most of Saturday to find something new to cook. The Sunday we visited she had made her usual light *madeleines* and *financiers* and the adrenalin rush was to be provided by experiments with brioche and crumble.

She needs no pointers on how to make tea, however. A true connoisseur, like many serious French tea drinkers, she has buying and serving it down to a fine art. The first golden rule of Hélène's teatime is always to serve a tea without *théine* (caffeine) usually an oolong. How inconsiderate it would be to spoil her guests' Sunday night's sleep! Making it all look beautiful is the second commandment. From her extensive travels in the Far East, Hélène has built a collection of exquisite teapots, tumblers and cups made from cast iron, finest porcelain and lacquered wood. She mixes and matches her favourite pieces, with a series of antique fabric print templates providing an equally colourful and intricate backdrop on the wall behind her table and chairs, picked up in a *brocante* (second-hand shop) a few streets away.

Everything is laid out ready for the guests, the idea being that they help themselves, in tune with the laid-back atmosphere. Invariably, however, Hélène cheerfully takes things in hand and serves those too shy to help themselves, or too engrossed in debate and comfortably wedged into her sofas.

Brioche

There are two secrets to making brioche. Firstly you must take your time; start the day before. Secondly, you need an electric mixer with a dough hook. This is a spectacular recipe which makes your house smell divine!

MAKES ONE LARGE BRIOCHE

500 g plain flour

50 g caster sugar

12.5 g fresh yeast

7 eggs

400 g butter at room temperature

1 egg yolk for glazing

3–4 crushed sugar lumps

2 teaspoons salt

The day before, between 3 and 5pm, put the flour, sugar and crumbled yeast in the mixer bowl and beat in 4 of the eggs.

Set up the dough hook. Turn the mixer on high and add the salt. Turn the mixer to medium speed and add the remaining 3 eggs, one by one. When the dough comes away from the sides of the bowl, gradually add the butter.

Keep mixing until the dough comes away from the sides of the bowl again. Pour it into a large floured baking bowl, cover with a tea-towel and put it in a warm undraughty place. Leave it alone for 2–3 hours.

When the dough has doubled its initial volume, crush it with your fist to its original size. Cover with clingfilm and put it in the fridge for 1 hour. Crush it again, cover and leave it in the fridge until the next day.

The following morning, take a ball of dough about the size of a tennis ball from the bowl and reserve. Put the rest of the dough in a buttered brioche mould and set the tennis ball on top. Leave to rise at room temperature for 1 hour.

Meanwhile, preheat the oven to 180°C/350°F/gas mark 4.

Brush the brioche all over with the egg yolk and sprinkle it with crushed sugar lumps. Cook for about 40 minutes.

Remove it from the mould and let it rest for about 1 hour before tasting. The yeast taste is too strong straight out of the oven.

Crumble aux fruits exotiques

Exotic fruit crumble

FOR 8–10

1 pineapple

40g butter, cold and cut into cubes

3 bananas

2 mangoes (frozen and peeled)

1 vanilla pod, split lengthways

4 tablespoons sugar

2 tablespoons rum

FOR THE CRUMBLE

125g plain flour

125g cold butter

125g brown sugar

80g dessicated coconut

Peel the pineapple, take out the hard middle part and cut it into chunks. In a saucepan, melt the butter and cook the pineapple for about 10 minutes. Add the bananas and mangoes, cut into thick slices. Add the vanilla seeds, the sugar and a little water if the fruit looks a bit dry. Generally the moisture from the mangoes is enough.

Preheat the oven to 180°C/350°F/gas mark 4.

Put the flour, butter, brown sugar and coconut in the bowl of your food-processor. Mix until the crumble forms. It should look like coarse breadcrumbs. Keep an eye on it in case it becomes lumpy. Put it in the fridge for 30 minutes. Mix the rum into the fruits.

Butter a gratin dish and sprinkle some sugar into it. Put the cooked fruit in and cover with the crumble. Cook for about 30 minutes until the crumble is golden.

Remove from the oven and allow to cool.

Madeleines et Financiers

Hélène insists on mentioning that these recipes are 'nicked' from her friends, author and cooking editor of Mme Figaro, Michèle Carles and the awesome *pâtissier*, Pierre Hermé. But whatever it is that Hélène does to them makes grown men and women cross Paris every Sunday to her home.

Financiers

MAKES 20 FINANCIERS

30 g butter for the moulds if you aren't using silicone ones
300 g caster sugar
A pinch of salt
160 g ground almonds
180 g softened butter
250 g plain flour, sifted
4 egg whites
A few drops of almond essence

Grease and flour 20 financier moulds, or find some magic silicone ones.

Preheat the oven to 150°C/300°F/gas mark 2.

Mix the sugar and salt with the almonds and set aside. Beat the softened butter with a wooden spoon until it becomes light and creamy. Beat the flour into the butter little by little.

Whisk the egg whites until they are stiff. Add the almond essence to the sugar and almonds and pour onto the egg whites. Then add this mixture to the butter and flour and mix well.

Divide the mixture between the moulds and cook for about 20 minutes until the cakes are golden and firm to the touch.

Madeleines

MAKES 20 MADELEINES

170 g butter
30 g butter for the moulds, see above
200 g plain flour, sifted
1 level teaspoon baking powder
5 eggs
200 g caster sugar
160 g ground almonds
A few drops of vanilla extract
The zest of 1 lemon
A pinch of salt

Melt the butter and leave it to cool (but not solidify). Grease and flour the madeleine moulds unless you have silicone versions.

Mix the flour, salt and baking powder.

In a bowl, beat the eggs with the sugar and ground almonds until the mixture turns white.

Preheat the oven to 200°C/400°F/gas mark 6.

With a whisk or a wooden spoon, add the flour gradually to the eggs and sugar, then the melted butter, vanilla extract and lemon zest. Stir well until the mixture is thick yet supple. Leave the batter to rest in a cool place for 15 minutes.

Fill each mould three-quarters full and cook for about 8–10 minutes. Remove from the oven; take the madeleines out of the moulds and leave to cool on a wire rack. Eat them immediately!

Conversion chart

Weight (solids)

7g	¼oz
10g	½oz
20g	¾oz
25g	1oz
40g	1½oz
50g	2oz
60g	2½oz
75g	3oz
100g	3½oz
110g	4oz (¼lb)
125g	4½oz
150g	5½oz
175g	6oz
200g	7oz
225g	8oz (½lb)
250g	9oz
275g	10oz
300g	10½oz
310g	11oz
325g	11½oz
350g	12oz (¾lb)
375g	13oz
400g	14oz
425g	15oz
450g	1lb
500g (½kg)	18oz
600g	1¼lb
700g	1½lb
750g	1lb 10oz
900g	2lb
1kg	2¼lb
1.1kg	2½lb
1.2kg	2lb 12oz
1.3kg	3lb
1.5kg	3lb 5oz
1.6kg	3½lb
1.8kg	4lb
2kg	4lb 8oz
2.25kg	5lb
2.5kg	5lb 8oz
3kg	6lb 8oz

Volume (liquids)

5ml	1 teaspoon
10ml	1 dessertspoon
15ml	1 tablespoon or ½floz
30ml	1floz
40ml	1½floz
50ml	2floz
60ml	2½floz
75ml	3floz
100ml	3½floz
125ml	4floz
150ml	5floz (¼pint)
160ml	5½floz
175ml	6floz
200ml	7floz
225ml	8floz
250ml (0.25 litre)	9floz
300ml	10floz (½pint)
325ml	11floz
350ml	12floz
370ml	13floz
400ml	14floz
425ml	15floz (¾pint)
450ml	16floz
500ml (0.5 litre)	18floz
550ml	19floz
600ml	20floz (1 pint)
700ml	1¼pints
850ml	1½pints
1 litre	1¾pints
1.2 litres	2 pints
1.5 litres	2½pints
1.8 litres	3 pints
2 litres	3½pints

Length

5mm	¼ inch
1cm	½ inch
2cm	¾ inch
2.5cm	1 inch
3cm	1¼ inch
4cm	1½ inch
5cm	2 inches
7.5cm	3 inches
10cm	4 inches
15cm	6 inches
18cm	7 inches
20cm	8 inches
24cm	10 inches
28cm	11 inches
30cm	12 inches

Glossary

Baies roses Literally pink berries, *baies roses* (once known as 'pink pepper') come from South America and have a pronounced taste with peppery, juniper and sweet aniseed notes. Great with fish (particularly scallops), white meats and even pan-fried foie gras.

Bain-marie A utensil for melting or heating ingredients (such as chocolate) without burning them. Can cool ingredients slowly also. Also used for keeping delicate sauces and mixtures warm. This double boiler-type utensil was originally used in alchemy.

Béchamel sauce A white sauce of milk added to a *roux* (see below). Goes well with egg, vegetable, pasta and gratin dishes. Used also as a basis for other sauces such as Mornay.

Beurre manié The French way of saying 'kneaded butter'; that is to say – equal amounts of softened butter and flour kneaded thoroughly. Used to thicken sauces and stews.

Beurre noisette A knob of butter heated to obtain a golden colour to accompany grilled fish and vegetables like spinach. Not to be confused with *beurre de noisette* which is grilled hazelnuts ground to a paste and bound with softened butter for use in sweet dishes like petits fours (sweet after-dinner morsels).

Bobo Means *bourgeois/bohemian*: upper-middle class, often corporate people with tolerant views of others, a significant disposable income who also manage to pass as bohemian. Bobos are descendants of the Yuppy.

Boudin noir Like an Irish black pudding or blood sausage, consists of seasoned pig's blood and fat contained in a length of intestine. Regional variations abound and every pork butcher has his own special recipe. This might mean the simple addition of raw or cooked onion, apple, bread or aromatic herbs.

Boucherie The place where meat is sold. In a word – a butcher's.

Boulangerie Where bread is made and sold.

Bouquet garni A little bundle of aromatic herbs – usually parsley, thyme and bay leaves – tied with string to prevent dispersal and used to flavour stocks or sauce. The contents of a bouquet garni change according to region. Shop-bought versions are often wrapped in muslin and mass-produced ones come packaged like tea bags.

Calvados / Pommeau Brandy made by distilling cider and left to mature in oak casks. Hails from Normandy and Brittany and drunk as a digestive. Used in cooking, particularly in dishes from Normandy. Pommeau is an alcoholic drink made in northern France by mixing unfermented cider and one-year-old Calvados. It is consumed as an apéritif, or as an accompaniment to melon or blue cheese. It is also popular with desserts, including any chocolate or apple-based dishes. Production of Calvados and Pommeau is very controlled.

Charcuterie Products made from pork and offal (sausages, pâtés, *boudin noir* etc.). The word also describes the shop where this kind of meat is sold. In France, charcuterie is particularly strong in the pig-rearing regions of Auvergne and Alsace.

Compote Normally fruit cooked and reduced in sugar. Can be served either warm or chilled flavoured with, say, vanilla, cloves or cinnamon and/or accompanied by cream and biscuits. Dried fruit soaked in water, tea or alcohol before cooking in a syrup can also constitute a compote, and vegetable compotes such as onion and pepper are common in France (although we would call them chutneys).

Crème fraîche épaisse Thick fresh cream. Obtained from pasteurised cows' milk, the thickness comes from the addition of a lactic bacteria culture that gives a sharp taste without souring it. Used endlessly in the kitchens of Normandy.

Eau de Vichy Sodium-rich water from Vichy – like the Vichy Saint-Yorre brand. Used principally in the kitchen to cook Carrots Vichy, a dish of sliced carrots cooked with the water and a little sugar. The cooked carrots absorb the sodium and are then tossed in butter and traditionally eaten as an accompaniment to veal cutlets or chicken.

Epicerie fine Fine grocer's shop. We'd call it a delicatessen.

Piment d'Espelette Espelette is a commune and small village in the Pyrénées-Atlantiques, known for its dried red peppers, used whole or ground to a hot powder. The peppers are designated as *Appellation d'Origine Contrôlée* and are hung to dry outside many of the houses and shops in the village during the summer.

Fleur de sel 'Flower of salt' is a hand-harvested sea salt collected by workers who scrape only the top layer of salt before it sinks to the bottom of large salt pans. Traditional French *fleur de sel* is collected off the coast of Brittany, and is slightly grey due to the sandy minerals that are collected in the process of harvesting the salt from the pans.

Fromagerie The place where cheese is sold.

Gros sel Coarse refined or unrefined salt, often grey in colour and used in cooking.

Haché Means finely chopped or minced.

Pâte sablée A crumbly pastry – used for making tartlets and *barquettes*, often filled with cream, fruit or jams. Shortcrust pastry to us.

Poitrine fumée Essentially 'smokey bacon' – although it comes as a thickish length of smoked, fatty pork belly that's cut into *lardons* (bacon cubes) for flavouring.

Reblochon A nutty-tasting, creamy-textured, cow's milk cheese made in Savoy with a pressed uncooked curd and a washed orange or pinky rind. Best eaten from May to October.

Rôtisserie The word has currency in English and means a shop or restaurant where spit-roast meat is prepared and sold. The word also applies to those electrically powered rotating spits designed for cooking meat and poultry both commercially and at home.

Roux A French/English dictionary will tell you that this word means a redhead. But as every housewife over 60 knows, a *roux* is that magic mix of equal parts flour and butter heated together (long enough to lose its floury taste) that constitutes the basis of many sauces including Béchamel and its derivatives (Mornay, Soubise etc.). Used for veloutés (see below), thickening gravy and rescuing a watery stew.

Traiteurs Literally caterer, but in France it has come to mean anyone selling prepared food – from the corner shop that sells cold-cooked ham to the legendary Fauchon, place de la Madeleine in Paris.

Tripier Person who sells the guts and innards (offal and tripe) from his tripe shop or *triperie*.

Velouté Velvety smooth and mellow sauce or soup. Usually made with a white chicken or veal stock thickened with a white *roux* (see above). Mushroom or chicken sauces and soups are basically veloutés, often with added cream. A direct translation might be 'cream of'…

Viande de grisons Dried beef – usually served in France in very thin slices.

Index

many thanks to

Kyle Cathie, Muna Reyal, Mary Evans and all the team for their extreme professionalism, cheerfulness and for keeping the faith long distance.

Ian and Ali, David and Margo Stevens and Iain and Ali Smith for letting me persistently fill their fridges with Sticky Toffee Pudding and clotted cream at very short notice.

My agent Ivan Mulcahy, in whose impressive brain the original idea of this book was born, for his sensitive and unfailing advice and support.

Odile Dupagne for the intro.

Alexandre Cammas and Le Fooding ® for helping to stir things up in Paris and give me lots to write home about.

Catherine Roig, Greg Delaney and Guillaume Crouzet for their invaluable commentaries and criticism.

Marie-Pierre Morel for taking exquisite pictures through the looking glass.

Garance, Lucy and Huguette, our lovely models.

Inaki Aizpitarte and all at Châteaubriand, Anne Daguin, Hélène Darroze, Joel Durand and Jean Luc Poujauran for their genius and everything about them that is French.

My suppliers in St-Germain-en-Laye: M. et Madame Bois Bernard, Sebastien Dubois, Stéphane Huet and everyone at La Marée.

Greg, Patric, Mado, Jean, Hélène, Gerald and Lou for the way they live their food.

Coco, Tim, Tanguy and Victoire. All my love always.

And to the chefs and restaurateurs:

Restaurant Hélène Darroze
4, rue d'Assas
75006 Paris
Tél: + 33 (0)1 42 22 00 11

Le Chateaubriand
129 avenue Parmentier
75011 Paris
Tél: + 33 (0)1 43 57 45 95

Le Petit Duc
7 boulevard Victor Hugo
13210 St Rémy de Provence,
Tél: + 33 (0)4 90 92 08 31

La Grande Duchesse
13 rue de Castellane
Paris 8 ème

Joel Durand
3 boulevard Victor Hugo
13210 Saint Remy de Provence
Tél: + 33 (0)4 90 92 38 25

acknowledgements

The author and publishers would also like to thank the following for their kind loan of props.

Astier de Villatte
173 rue du faubourg Saint-Honoré
75001 Paris
Tél: + 33 (0)1 42 60 74 13
www.astierdevillatte.com

Bernardaud
11 rue Royale
75008 Paris
Tél: + 33 (0)1 43 12 52 00
www.bernardaud.fr

Cuisinophilie
28 rue du Bourg-Tibourg
75004 Paris
Tél: + 33 (0)1 40 29 07 32

107 Rivoli
107 rue de Rivoli
75001 Paris
Tél: + 33 (0)1 42 60 64 94

Gien
18 rue de l'Arcade
75008 Paris
Tél: + 33 (0)1 42 66 52 32
www.gien.com

Le Creuset
www.lecreuset.fr